HOW TO
MAKE
BIRDIES!

John Gollehon

GOLLEHON BOOKS™
GRAND RAPIDS, MICHIGAN

Library of Congress Catalog Card Number 2004102019

ISBN 0-914839-74-8
(International Standard Book Number)

GOLLEHON BOOKS are published by: Gollehon Press, Inc.,
6157 28th St. SE, Grand Rapids, MI 49546.

GOLLEHON BOOKS are available in quantity purchases; contact
Special Sales. Gollehon does not accept unsolicited manuscripts.
Brief book proposals are reviewed.

Contents

About the author

John Gollehon is the founder of Gollehon Golf, a maker of golf clubs and training aids. Many of the clubs manufactured are sold under the Gollehon name. An avid golfer for over 45 years, his research into the methods and nuances of teaching the game over the years has been an equally enjoyable pastime, providing the impetus for *How To Make Birdies!*

This book is dedicated to golfers of all levels.

Those who just want to get the ball in the air, and those who want to win the U.S. Open.

And all golfers in between.

CHAPTER 1

A New Way To Improve Your Game!

"There are two things that won't last long in this world, and that's dogs chasing cars and pros putting for pars."
—Lee Trevino

Here's a statistic that you might find hard to believe: Over 95 percent of all golfers do not significantly improve their game. Once they've reached a certain level of play, it's as if they've accepted it as par for the course. But they haven't fully resigned themselves to the idea that they'll never win the club championship. Otherwise, how do you explain all those full sets of old clubs in the corner of the garage? Sure, a new set of high-tech clubs is the easy way to improve that handicap.

That's the thinking. And that thinking is wrong. What you are more likely to accomplish with that new set of clubs is putting another "old" set of clubs on the block for next spring's garage sale.

The hordes of hackers who populate the 18,993 golf courses around the country (you really can't mean it when you say you're having trouble getting a tee-time!) would *like* to be better golfers, but only a select few actually make significant improvements. Hard to believe, isn't it? But it's true. Handicap statistics bear it out. If you're a 20 handicapper, you might see 18. If you're a 15, you might see 13. Or worse, you might see your scores begin to ride up in spite of all the hours you spend on the range practicing your mistakes until they become second-nature to you. Golfers do that. Lesson after lesson, and they go right back to their "old" game.

The "Elixir" Syndrome

You should know right up front that this book is for serious golfers. I'm talking about golfers who are never satisfied with their level of skill. Always looking for that one great tip from a club pro, maybe even a playing partner, one little suggestion to fix one simple little flaw in the fundamentals that will make that ball fly 275 yards straight as an arrow… *consistently*.

Golf lessons are up exponentially. Golf schools run by the best teachers in the land have long waiting lists, in spite of the hefty costs. Hey, if you have to go to the hospital you want the best doctor, right? So why would it be any different with golf? You want the best because you want results. You know the hard reality, but you're on a mission: to defeat the golf gods who sneak in and screw up your game.

As I alluded to at the top of this chapter, the idea that new high-tech clubs will cure all your ills is rammed into our brains by club manufacturers who must have the best hype artists this side of Madison Avenue. They have to. Every year at the PGA Merchandise Show in Orlando, the big guns gather to show off their new clubs for the upcoming season. New clubs that are better than last year's new clubs. The first thing that customers ask as they walk into an exhibitor's booth is, "What's new?" And there better be something new (and improved) or that club manufacturer is in for a long season.

Other indicators today of this strange paradox among golfers are swing aids and putting aids and all the other Rube Goldberg contraptions on the market. Anything that will take strokes off your game is selling like maps to a secret treasure. For that's what they really are. Something short of the secrets of life, but not that short. No sir! Finding the secrets to improving your golf game is serious business.

We all know who dangles the carrot on the stick that leads us on. The pros. Every time we watch a pro tournament, we can't help but wonder why we're all making such a big deal out of what should be gosh-awful easy. The swing is nice and smooth. The tempo is like slow-motion. The ball travels straight and far and bounces a few feet from the pin. "A piece of cake! I can do that!" you exclaim. "All I have to do is just keep my head down. Yeah, that's it. The whole problem here is with my head."

Well, if you think it's that easy to hit a shot like the pros, you're right. The problem *is* with your head. There is no elixir in a bottle that is going to take your game to the pro level. But no one should tell you that it can't be done. I'm certainly not going to. Take it in steps; take it in stride. You must have the patience and desire to get there.

There's an interesting psyche to this crowning achievement. When it happens, if it happens, it might completely change you. All of a sudden you can hit the ball like a pro. Wow! There's tremendous satisfaction in hitting the ball straight and long. For some, it's even a measure of self-worth. That's right. It's that important. And you know if you fit the bill if you watch the Golf Channel for umpteen hours each day, play in driving rainstorms, or carry four wedges in your bag. Face it. It may not be every day but there *are* days when the world spins around golf.

We've all been there, haven't we? Think about it. You just wrote your biggest contract at work, landed your biggest customer... name your accomplishment, so you take the rest of the day off, go to the club, and fire a 73. We should probably tell everyone that you *used to be* a 15 handicapper.

At the nineteenth hole, what's the first thing you tell your friends? When you get home, what's the first thing you tell your spouse? If I know golfers, you'll spend 15 minutes going over every shot en route to that beautiful 73. The contracts? The big customer? What? Oh, that!

Just the thought of shooting a near-par round of golf is all the encouragement any high-handicapper needs to try another route to get there. They forget all those dead-ends and welcome any new tactic that might work. A new training aid, more practice, more lessons. Whatever.

So let me tell you more about the route I want you to try next. It's an old road but it hasn't seen much travel in years.

I want you to take more lessons. That's what this book is about. But what's different about this book is who's going to teach you.

Masters Of The Game

So what's the best way to take strokes off your game? To achieve that seemingly impossible dream? I think I've got the best answer, but you'll have to let me qualify it, especially if you're a young golfer, not entirely familiar with surnames such as Sarazen, Demaret, or Mangrum. But certainly you recognize Snead, Hogan, Jones, or Hagen? Come on! Even weekend duffers have heard of *those* guys!

In the next chapter we'll begin lessons from these "masters of the game." But for now, I want to make sure that you can appreciate the value of what you are about to learn. So let's make some comparisons. Let's compare equipment. And let's compare the courses. We need a level playing field if we're going to compare the expertise of the old masters to today's standouts.

No one would argue that the equipment today is far superior to what was available in the '40s, '50s, and '60s, the years when great strides were made in the refinement and resultant popularity of the game. Forget light-weight titanium drivers and perimeter-weighted, investment-cast irons. Solid persimmon heads could hit the golf ball a decent distance, but only if you found the "sweet spot," and only if every muscle was perfectly synchronized to develop power in such a relatively heavy club.

The weak link among clubs, however, was clearly the irons. Putters, on the other hand, were decent tools to sink putts. Over the years, there is little that technology has done to improve a putter. You either have the right line and the right speed or you don't.

To prove the point, I recently watched as a club pro ventured off to the driving range with a set of clubs from the early '60s and a brand new set from a top-name manufacturer. He hit the real woods within 15 yards of today's metal woods. "You just have to swing slower," he said.

The old irons were the toughest to hit and provided the most telling inadequacies from today's offerings. So, the next time you watch an old film of Slammin' Sammy popping a 3-iron to within a few feet of the pin, I hope you'll appreciate it even more.

On the putting green, there was little difference in results. New putters, old putters. They all seemed to perform about the same. Surprised?

Now about those courses they played. Greens were unpredictable. Some fairways were no different from today's first cut of rough.

Thanks to the USGA's staff of agronomists, today's courses are works of art.

And we haven't even talked about the sand. Oh, what a difference a few decades can make!

Sure, we all have great respect for today's pro golfers and instructors. But I think you'll agree with me that learning the game from the pros who fought with all they had on the front lines of adversity is a better way to go. You want to learn a tough game? Learn it from the tough!

The next two chapters are titled "Setup Basics" and "Swing Basics." The operative word is "basics." There are a few basics that you absolutely must adhere to. Not a lot, just a few. Let's not make this more difficult than it really is! It really is... basic!

Why Make It Complicated?

Watching a foursome of top golf instructors on a popular television program, I was tuned in like every other rabid golfer, hanging on every word. After all, it's not often that such a lustrous group of teaching pros get together for a jam session. But you know what? I left the program a bit confused. As I'm sure other golfers did. Clearly, these guys were not on the same page. It seemed as if they all had their own "manual of style" for hitting a golf ball.

The sheer volume of advice, sometimes conflictive, made my head swim. And I wondered how it could be that such great variations in advice could produce such remarkable uniformity among today's professional players.

Could it be that today's teaching methods are best fitted for the pro level, and not particularly helpful for the average player?

If your golf pro tells you to "do this, don't do that," you can pretty much understand the scope of these simple instructions. After all, we learned what "do this, don't do that" means by the time we got to kindergarten. Don't pull a girl's dress up, don't shoot spit balls, *do* keep your desk clean, *do* raise your hand when you have to go pee. In other words, don't just pee. OK, so maybe it wasn't *that* easy.

But what do you do when one instructor tells you to keep your left heel down, and then another instructor interrupts and says you shouldn't be afraid to lift it up? Who's right here?! (We'll learn the answer in the next chapter.)

And what about gripping the club? One guy said to hold the club lightly but firmly. Taking a cue from Sam Snead, he added, "Hold it as if you are holding a bird."

"Not so fast," says pro No. 2, taking a cue from Lee Corso. "That doesn't work with all shots. You have to hold it tightly when you're hitting out of a trap, or if your ball is in heavy rough. Otherwise, the grass (or sand) will turn the clubface before you strike the ball." Hmm.

One pro spent five minutes talking about the importance of the right elbow; another pro finally cut him off by saying that it wasn't important. "The *left* arm is what we should be talking about," he said. Hmm.

I also noticed something during the program that may have escaped the attention of other viewers. None of the pros used the same terminology. My favorite teaching pro always used the term *takeaway* when talking about the basic swing. Another pro called it the *backswing*. It was also referred to as the *backstroke*, the *takeback*, and the *upswing*. Huh?!*

These pros would often preface what they were about to say with, "The way I teach..." suggest-

---

*In this book, we'll use the terms *backswing* and *downswing*. The "takeaway," incidentally, is the first stage of the backswing.

ing, of course, that they all teach somewhat differently. And guess what? They do.

It's a good thing these guys are golf instructors and not kindergarten teachers. I mean, you can't say "pee" one minute and "wee-wee" the next. You can't tell a kid he can't pull up Jane's dress, but it's OK to look up.

No. It's not OK to look up. You have to keep your head dead still. Every golfer knows that. We all learned it in kindergarten.

A Set Of Standards

The pros I've talked to would like to see a set of standards established in the art of teaching the game. There are few. There are as many different ways to teach the basic swing as there are instructors. Well, maybe that's an exaggeration, but not much of one.

Many pros today rely on video equipment as an aid to teaching. But just exactly how effective is seeing your swing in a zillion different increments? And then there's the issue of personalized one-on-one instruction falling by the wayside. Some pros like to teach in classes. That's right. Class instruction is a trend that's making inroads across the country.

Great! Just what you need. Twenty-two golfers asking 22 different questions, all at the same time. I think we went through this in kindergarten.

So what about these new trends?

I remember a comment Greg Norman made recently when talking about one of his favorite instructors and particularly this gentleman's old-school way of teaching. Let me paraphrase Norman as he compared the technique of his old friend to today's high-tech instruction. Norman said, "It's video cameras today, from all angles, and recorders and monitors with stop-action and slow-mo that make it all too complex. The old-school way is to teach what a good swing *feels* like. Not what it looks like."

I love the quote; it speaks volumes. Everyone would like to have a swing like Greg Norman. Effortless, smooth-as-silk, and just darn-right beautiful to look at. But who's kidding whom? The only golfer with a Greg Norman swing is Greg Norman.

Besides, there are thousands of different swings that can get the job done. And isn't that more important than looking like someone else? Personally, I'd take Lee Trevino's loopy swing, or Jim Thorpe's, or Jim Furyk's, and I'd even offer to help them carry their money to the bank! **As hard as it is for amateurs to accept, it's not the swing that counts, it's the result.**

This whole discussion reminds me of an old pro I used to play with who had a goofy backswing, and an annoying hesitation at the top, but in that last third of the downswing you could just see the power unleash. "You know the instant you strike the ball if you've hit a good shot," he would always say. And don't we all know that? If it feels like the golf ball is made of butter, you can't wait to look up and admire your good shot. But don't we also know what it feels like to smack a chunk of concrete?

Swing Personality

You'll see more swing variations on the Champion's Tour than the regular tour, and you'll see even more unusual swings if you watch film of the old-time pros from decades long past. Why? Because, for the most part, these champions of their day taught themselves.

Personally, I'd much rather learn from the true inventors and experimenters of the golf swing than from the rash of teachers today who preach the same swing, the same way, the only way. It's called Method Golf, and it's the last time you'll hear that term in this book. **We are not automatons. We are unique individuals who will produce unique swings.**

All we ask for are the basic fundamentals that will help us within the framework of our own individuality. But it doesn't seem to be happening. Particularly at the college ranks and on the Nationwide Tour, you'll be hard-pressed to recognize a golfer by his or her swing.

In the old days, there was virtually no bickering among the pros about the fundamentals. But the execution of a good golf swing was as unique as the players themselves. And these distinctly different swings garnered the respect to be left alone. More than that, they gave the tour players an instantly identifiable swing. It gave them a swing "personality."

And here's what's important to note: **The teaching pros of that era were smart enough to know that they dare not change these individual styles. Fundamentals are one thing; idiosyncrasies are another.**

Subtle Changes

It's remarkable how subtle changes can make significant improvement to your game. Everyone's game. Everyone's swing. Rest assured that the subtle tips you are about to learn, sometimes hidden in today's teachings of the game, will work on all kinds of swings. A good teacher today, as in the old days, should look past the superficial, unimportant "flaws" of your swing and look deeper into the fundamentals. Quite often, the "fix" is a simple adjustment.

Indeed. You probably don't need a complete makeover. Drastic changes are not the order of this book. Making a radical "adjustment" can sometimes hurt your game beyond repair. Who doesn't have a story to tell about a golfer-friend who's still trying to recoup from the lessons he took months earlier? **Today's teachers of the game from club pros to the top nationally recognized instructors should follow the physician's creed: First do no harm.**

Many instructors, frankly, still have not learned that subtle changes may be the correct course of action. Subtle changes can make a huge difference in your game. Best of all, subtle changes are usually easy to make.

And that's the gist of this book. From the tee to the cup, you'll learn subtle changes to make that will accomplish the task. The task? Oh, yes. We have one goal in mind. And it is exactly as the book title so aptly defines. We are going to learn how to make more birdies.

Every single tip, every little nuance, is geared to getting your ball on the green and ready for a birdie putt. And I'm not talking a 30-footer for birdie. The idea is to get your ball in position for a *makeable* birdie putt. Let's say within 12 feet. Makeable. At 40 feet you're not really putting for birdie; you'll be happy with a 2-putt for par.

These subtle changes we're going to make to your game were preached day-in and day-out by golf's best, sans video camera and high-tech clubs and perfect courses. The advice you'll read is from a consensus of the top players who helped to pioneer the teaching trail before golf instruction became so complicated. Players like Gene Sarazen, Ben Hogan, and Bobby Jones.

Jones, for example was a voracious writer about the basic fundamentals. And he provided hours upon hours of film instruction. We should all be thankful that his valuable advice has been saved for generations to come. It will not grow old. It will not become passé. Why? Because he concentrated on the subtleties of the game. And he kept it simple. Any golf instructor who didn't is not included in these pages.

This is a unique book. Vastly different from all the other teaching books on golf. Nothing heavy, nothing complicated. Remember, it's mostly the subtle changes that will make the significant difference you're looking for. You'll understand and appreciate the power of subtlety almost immediately.

Here's a chart that lists the pros who have been referenced in this book. Since many of the names will not be familiar to all readers, an accompanying list of their major wins, and the dates of those wins, are included.

PLAYER	EVENT	YEAR
Gay Brewer	The Masters	1967
Billy Casper	U.S. Open	1959, 1966
	The Masters	1970
Jimmy Demaret	The Masters	1940, 1947, 1950
Doug Ford	PGA Championship	1955
	The Masters	1957
Ben Hogan	U.S. Open	1948, 1950, 1951, 1953
	PGA Championship	1946, 1948
	The Masters	1951, 1953
	British Open	1953
Bobby Jones	U.S. Open	1929, 1930
	British Open	1926, 1927, 1930
Lloyd Mangrum	U.S. Open	1946
Byron Nelson	U.S. Open	1939
	PGA Championship	1940, 1945
	The Masters	1937, 1942
Gene Sarazen	U.S. Open	1922, 1932
	PGA Championship	1922, 1923, 1933
	The Masters	1935
	British Open	1932
Sam Snead	PGA Championship	1949, 1951
	The Masters	1949, 1952, 1954
	British Open	1946

CHAPTER 2
Setup Basics

"Golf is a compromise between what
your ego wants you to do, what
experience tells you to do, and what
your nerves *let* you do."

—*Bruce Crampton*

Of all the intricate aspects of the golf swing, the way a player addresses the ball is by far the most varied. Even the advice of the Old Masters is surprisingly varied, too. Suffice it to say, it was difficult to find a consensus among the top legends of the game.

Addressing the ball meant many different things in years past, from Art Carney's unforgettable "Hello-o-o ball!" to Ben Hogan's quirky "left foot turned out, right foot square" routine. I mean, who does that today?!

If you watch today's top players carefully, you'll notice that their setups are remarkably varied, also. But the fundamentals, for the most part, are solid.

The Right Grip

Every pro, today and yesterday, will tell you the importance of the right grip. But what exactly *is* the right grip? Many of today's pros do not grip the club in textbook fashion, which makes a beginner wonder just exactly how important the grip is. Obviously, it is important to have a grip that works. But I believe it's fair to say that there is considerable room for variations.

A strong grip has the left hand turned far to the right so that the first knuckle is nearly on top of the club. A weak grip has the left hand turned too far to the left with the thumb resting naturally on the very top of the club. **With a strong grip, the clubhead doesn't turn through the swing. There is little concern about squaring up the clubface for that moment of impact. It essentially *stays* square.**

A weak grip, however, generally means the right hand is turned too far to the left, creating at least three problems:

(1) an improper feeling that the right hand and arm are dominant,

(2) an open clubface at impact that could create a slice, and

(3) a nagging tendency to "come over the ball," swinging from outside in.

Of the two "wrong" grips, clearly the strong grip produces the least problems. Personally, I've had a strong grip since I was a kid. I couldn't change it now if I wanted to. Not surprisingly after all these years, my grip is not a problem. I've molded my swing to fit the strong grip. But golfers just starting out, particularly young golfers, should learn the right way to grip a golf club.

Golf instruction books spend page after page describing the proper grip. As I perused the current market of books and compared information to the wisdom of the old pros, I must admit that I was overwhelmed with conflicting advice, not to mention confusing tips, until I re-read Harvey Penick's *Little Red Book*.

He says, "Pick up a yardstick and let your hands fit it." He says that's the way to grip a club. No wonder Penick was such an admired teacher. He kept it simple. He would never overwhelm a student.

Your Hands Must Work As One Unit

There are several different ways to "connect" your hands around the club once you've learned how the hands relate to each other with Penick's well-known "yardstick" trick. The most common, and most preferred way, is to simply allow your little finger of your right hand to fall into the groove between the first and second finger of your left hand. That's it. Simple enough?

There's one other thing worth noting about the basic grip, and that's the tendency of some rookie players to put too much feel into the right thumb and first finger, as if they're using them to help guide the club. In fact, Hogan taught players to practice with the right thumb and first finger completely removed from the club. This unusual practice tip would help a beginning golfer realize that these two appendages are somewhat neutral.

But what's more remarkable about this practice tip is the different feeling one gets in the remaining fingers. You'll quickly learn what a "connected" grip feels like. **The hands must feel as if they are working in tandem, as one unit, not two units joined together.**

It's an important point in my particular case, and perhaps other golfers as well. Until just a few years ago, I would catch myself placing my right thumb squarely on top of the club to help guide it, I guess, and relying too much on the right first finger to both steady my grip and provide strength.

It's a bad move for several reasons, not the least of which is the wear and tear on the pad of your thumb caused by the friction against the rubber grip. Several times I'd look down at my right thumb and find it cracked and bleeding. I wanted to keep my thumb on the club (after all, I'd been doing it for so long) so I eventually began wearing a bandage over my thumb pad. Today, I know how much trouble I can get into with my thumb on top and my first finger squeezing the club. And I now have a better sense that the power and control are coming from my left hand.

Sure, the last three fingers of your right hand are important, too, if you want to maintain a balanced feeling of connection. But concentrate on the left hand (and arm, for that matter) as you progress through your swing.

Other pros of Hogan's era would preach that the grip, the *combined* grip, must feel as if the hands are bound to the club, producing a solid coupling that extends the club shaft through the hands to the arms.

These pros believed that the feel of the golf swing came from the fingers. It seems elementary to think so, but you'd be surprised how many golfers incorrectly place the club more in the palms of the hands rather than the fingers. **The fingers hold the club. The fingers provide the feel of the swing.**

Balance

The club is positioned to the ball first, then the feet are positioned. Sam Snead was adamant about this procedure. **"You never position your feet and then the clubhead."**

Once you have positioned yourself in relation to the ball, gripping and regripping to get just the right feel in the hands, you have three more important things to do before you take a swipe at that ball that's been staring at you for the past few seconds. Well, the ball will always be ready. It's you who must make *yourself* ready.

Do you feel balanced in your stance? **The weight of your body should be distributed equally on the balls of your feet... not your heels, not your toes. Your feet should be spaced at shoulder width, maybe a little more, rarely less*.** Sometimes you'll see pros on the tee positioning and repositioning their feet to the

---

*Technically, the width of your stance will vary with the club you use, your height, and even your weight. But a shoulder-wide stance is a good rule in general.

ground much as they do their hands to the grip. The reasons are clear: relaxation, comfort, and balance. Call it a preparation to strike.

The knees are slightly flexed. The bend in your body comes from the waist. You don't stoop over the ball. Your arms are hung straight down from your shoulders. You don't reach out to the ball. Your head is dead still. And you know you must keep it dead still throughout the entire backswing and downswing or all bets are off. A waggle or two and you're ready to unleash.

A Favorite Golfing Wisdom

No matter how thorough the description of a good setup, it's doubtful that most everyday golfers really have the picture in their minds of exactly what they want their bodies to do, and it's doubtful that all the right muscles have been placed on alert, ready to move in perfect sequence and harmony to deliver the perfect golf shot.

So, let me share with you one of my favorite wisdoms from the often-quoted Abe Mitchell, an old English pro who seemed to have a knack for explaining the difficult. Mitchell said, "A golfer must always move freely beneath himself."

Even though the swing itself is saved for the next chapter, the *thought* of the swing (and the shot) is, indeed, a part of a golfer's setup. And what better way to understand what is about to happen, and to prepare for it, than to fully visualize Mitchell's magical maxim.

Can you picture in your mind exactly what Mitchell is talking about? Every action you take is referenced to a fixed point... your head. The club orbits in a swing plane around your spine, an extension down from your head. Your hips and legs drive through the ball, powered to move freely, but turning (not swaying) on an axis that extends from your head. **Your head doesn't contribute to the power; it *controls* the power.**

Tips & Tricks:
Subtle Changes That Can Help
Your Setup

The left hand:

Think of your left hand as being in charge of the swing. You don't want to grip any more firmly with the left hand, but you do want to be sure that the grip doesn't weaken at the top of the backswing... a frequent problem with high handicap players that will cost you distance and control. To emphasize the importance of the left hand, it's interesting to note that some golfers with power-ful swings actually lose their right-hand grip after the moment of impact. It's as if the left hand is pulling with so much power that the right hand can't keep up.

Ball position on the tees:

(1) Play your drives off the inside of your left foot so that you catch the ball just at the begin-ning of the upswing. It will help you get the ball in the air. If you frequently slice, try playing the ball a little farther to the left, which means the clubface will be slightly turned in at contact. You may have to tee the ball slightly higher.

Take slow practice swings and note at which points (relative to your left foot position) your clubface remains open, becomes square, and be-gins turning inward. If you're striking the ball be-fore the clubface has reached its square position (and has yet to reach the target line), you are vir-tually assured of a push or slice.

(2) Play your irons on par 3 holes near the cen-ter of your stance (or slightly behind) so that the club strikes the ball on the downswing. You must hit down on the ball to impart spin that will help the ball hold the green. Tee the ball low or don't use a tee. Many players don't. You might take a

divot, loose dirt, or just brush the grass, but this should occur *after* the ball is airborne. If you strike the ground behind the ball, your ball position is too far forward, or you're swaying to the right side (a reverse pivot) during your backswing.

Curing the sway:

There are two remedies for this problem, a dichotomy of opposing advice. Try a slightly wider stance that might help to provide more stability. The right foot extended slightly outward serves as a brace against movement. The downside of a wider stance is a tendency to lose power in the downswing.

Or, try the opposite—a narrow stance would suggest that you would lose your balance if you sway, and you would have to stop in mid-swing. Either of these tips should help prevent swaying, but the best way to stop it is to keep your head still. No up and down. No side to side.

There's actually a third attack to the problem although it would be more appropriately found in the next chapter. Concentrate on the weight distribution to your feet, being sure that your weight never shifts beyond the inside of your right foot.

Aligning your shot:

If I didn't tell you about the age-old trick to assuring alignment, I'd be the only golf writer who missed it. Everyone preaches it exactly the same way. Technology just hasn't kept up, I guess.

Place a long iron across your toes after you've established your setup. Then, take a few steps away from the target and look at the direction the long iron is pointing.* Is it pointing toward the target or are you aiming toward the woods? When I gave my wife lessons years ago, alignment was the one thing she couldn't master. No trick in the book could help her. She just had a poor sense of direction.

Incidentally, I don't recommend giving your spouse lessons if you value your marriage. Leave this thankless job to the pros at your club. And if you find out that your favorite pro has been married four times, now you know why.

---

*This advice assumes that your feet are equidistant from the target line. If you pull back your left or right foot, placing a long iron across your toes will *not* give you the right target line. In such cases, have a friend place the iron across your shoulders as a means of alignment. Of course, your friend will have to tell you if you are aligned correctly.

Since there are golfers who can square up their lower body but distort the alignment of the upper body during setup (usually because of a sideways bend at the waist), the shoulder alignment concept can help square up the entire body.

Accentuating the positive:

If ever there was a consensus among top in-structors from years past, it was the importance of psyching yourself into the shot. No negative thoughts. No thoughts at all, in fact. Except one: the picture in your mind of the ball flying exactly as you want it to. Clear your head and let your programmed swing do the job.

It's great advice, isn't it? But not the easiest to pull off. Case in point:

A golfer I used to play with allowed a different picture to float into his mind whenever there was a group of golfers behind us waiting at our tee. If we were in a foursome, there were now seven players watching every little twitch this guy would make standing up there on the tee-box, as if it were a stage. And he couldn't get those seven pairs of eyes on him out of his head.

It's also why he never liked to play through a group. To him, it just meant more people watching him hit. Every time we played through together, he hit the worst tee-shot imaginable. Clearing his head was impossible. I know. I tried to get him to do it for years. But as soon as he learned to con-centrate on the right picture—the positive picture—a picture of the golf ball performing miraculous things, he hit it just fine. All he needed was something positive to concentrate on.

A positive mode can mean more than just pictures in your mind. It can also be reflected in the positive way that you present yourself as you prepare for each shot. Another case in point:

Bobby Jones used to follow a strict procedure every time he walked onto a tee. After he teed the ball, he would walk back a few steps and look at the target, visualizing the shot he wanted to make. He walked back to the ball with the confidence that he could make that shot.

Taking his stance, he would not dally, for he found that the more time he spent over the ball, the more often that trouble would ensue.

Good advice, right? Besides, no one wants to play with a guy who goes through 23 seconds worth of waggles and gripping exercises every time he sticks a tee in the ground. It's either a goofy habit or a sign of indecisiveness.

Remember, think positive, and get on with it.

Every pro golfer has a routine that they follow religiously on the tees. Do you?

Talking about Bobby Jones reminded me of an important aspect in the setup that few players today subscribe to. When it's their turn to hit, they may take a practice swing, maybe two, they might look at the target from the setup position, they might look again just before they strike the ball. Sometimes they take a practice half-swing; sometimes a full swing. Sometimes at full speed, sometimes not. The number of waggles and the way they do it varies from tee to tee. Suffice it to say, there is no routine, no regimen, no standard operating procedure. And that's widely regarded as a bad thing. Here's why:

Your own routine—once established and always followed—will help give you confidence. It's as if every course you play is your home course. That's right. It gives you a home field advantage! You take it with you everywhere you play.

You know exactly what you're going to do the moment you walk up on the tee. No fidgeting, no hurried motions, no confusion, no fears, and no forgetting of an important piece of your routine. You won't forget to stand behind the ball and look at your target, for example... a trait that should be a part of every golfer's arsenal.

Pick a "trigger" to start the backswing. It could be something as simple as cocking your head to the right as Nicklaus does, or that nifty half-swing that Weir performs. Most golfers turn the key on the second or third waggle. Whatever action you decide upon, understand that the idea is to prevent you from starting your swing from a stopped position. In fact, you should never find yourself "stuck" over the ball.

You will gain confidence from an established routine within just a few holes. Trust me.

Fixing problems in the setup:

It has always amazed me how many problems can be fixed just by changing something in your setup.

Golfers who have trouble with a full hip turn on the downswing can get a boost by turning the left foot slightly outward. In this position, the body turn is easier to make and provides more clearance for the proper arm and hand action.

If you're one of the many golfers who slice or hook their drives, try moving away from a square stance, allowing your feet position to help you straighten out your shots.

(1) Slicers can drop their right foot back two or three inches, increasing the ease of a full shoulder turn and encouraging an inside-out swing.

(2) Dropping your left foot back two or three inches encourages a fade, but also opens the door to an outside-in swing, which could create a slice.

Top of the arms tight to the chest, elbows in:

It's one of Hogan's most important teachings. Although there is some current debate, I must mention it here because the advice has produced the most significant improvement to my own game. Hopefully, you'll find that it improves your game, too.

At setup, literally press the upper section of your arms against your chest. But not tightly, of course. At the top of your swing, the left arm remains against your chest while your right arm naturally moves outward (don't fly the elbow). The upper arms brush the chest through the downswing.

Now about those elbows. They should be held closely together, but not to the point of producing tension in your forearms. At a minimum, there should be no bend. Speaking from experience, I can tell you that it feels awkward to make this change if you've always let your elbows stick out at setup. Get used to pressing them as close together as practical without feeling any sort of stress.

The idea is that by keeping your elbows close together, you've created a strong, solid extension of the club all the way to your shoulders. And by keeping your upper arms loosely

against your chest, you'll hit the ball squarely on the sweet spot because there is less chance for retracting or extending the radius of the swing arc.*

Equally important, the feeling of a solid connection... that is, the arms and hands operating as a solid unit, is quite dramatic.

In my own case, I use a variation on Hogan's advice for the elbows at setup. I have little choice because it is too difficult for me to position my elbows as he advised in view of my strong grip. And, frankly, I like my way of extending my arms (the net effect of bringing the elbows close together) because the change I created helps me in another area, too. Here's my way of using Hogan's recommendation:

Instead of positioning the clubface behind the ball and close to the ground as one would normally do, I position the clubface so that it is about two inches above the ground. It stays to the right of

---

* Even seasoned golfers are subject to this problem of retracting or extending the swing radius. The centrifugal force of a golf swing can easily extend your arms outward, creating ball contact on the heel of the clubface, or, God forbid, on the shaft or hosel. And you know what that means: SHANK! Sometimes the clubface is pulled back because of movement in the shoulders or simply a weight shift to the heels. You'll either hit the ball off the toe, or, God forbid, miss the whole tamale. And you know what that means: WHIFF!

the ball; I simply position it as if it were raised straight up. A few waggles, a couple of head turns to the target, and I'm ready to pull my trigger.

The trigger is simply dropping the clubface into position with the extension of my arms. I'm careful not to make any other body changes. The extra couple of inches come from the straightening out of my arms.

Of course, I don't hold that position so I don't feel any stress. As I said, that move is my trigger, so the instant I drop the club into position, I'm ready to start the backswing.

The venerable "V's":

An old leather-bound book about golf, published in London in 1934, was one of many period books I dusted off, looking for tidbits of advice to incorporate into my manuscript. Actually, I probably chose to read it because these old beauties are a pure delight to read, particularly if you're into the history of the game.

Anyhow, I remember a tip that caught my attention from this now-nondescript author about the different grips used by European players of that era. The writer said that he was not so concerned about the actual placement of the hands on the club as he was about the relative location of the V's formed by the thumb and first finger of each hand.

He said that the only important concern about the grip a player takes is that these V's point in parallel lines.

Hmm. I remembered reading that very same tip in some other publication during the six months that I did research for my book. Someone had said that the V's should match up, pointing in the same direction, whether a strong grip or a weak grip, an interlocking, overlapping, or baseball grip. Just pay attention to your V's.

Well, I couldn't find this other mention, important in my quest to publish only consensus advice. And then, weeks later, I was skimming through a stack of recent golf magazines and there I found it. That same tip was published 70 years later in a current golf magazine!

I don't like cliches, but there's a most appropriate one for this revelation:

> "The more things change,
> the more things stay the same."

CHAPTER 3
Swing Basics

"If you want to play better golf, always play with golfers better than you are."
—*John Gollehon*

Golf: A Love-Hate Relationship

Let me ask a question to all 20 and higher handicappers. How many times have you thought about quitting the game? It's a legitimate question, and I have good reason for asking.

There are more times than not when the frustrations can overpower the pleasures of golf. And when that happens, it's only logical to start thinking about bowling or billiards to replace golf as that recreational pastime that you always looked so forward to. If you live in a retirement community, and you're too old to chase women, there's always shuffleboard, I guess. You're thinking, *Hmm, this might be tougher than I thought.*

Here's the way the scenario almost always plays out. You're on the course with your friends. They are all having a great round. You, however, are struggling. It's time to reach into that bag again to find a ball while mumbling something like, "Damn water!" You fish around in the very depths of a very deep pocket and all you can find are range balls. You're thinking, *Well, I can always bum a freakin' ball from someone*, but, alas, you find the one you never play because it's so cut up and dirty that no respectable ball-washer would even accept it!

So you trudge on, moving your head all over the place, swinging wildly with your arms, trying to kill that ugly dirt-caked thing with dimples and a big smile just to put it out of its misery.

Yep, it's time to sell the bag and clubs and find a real hobby that you can enjoy. You know you'll take a hit on the clubs—you paid $800 for the irons, $400 for the big driver that did absolutely nothing for your game. The bag's a throw-in. *Let's see*, you're thinking, *maybe I can get three hundred if I put an ad in the paper.*

And just think of all the money you'll save: no more dues, no dining minimums, no cart fees, no range fees or locker fees, no more bag storage fees, either. You wonder if you're playing at a club or at a bank!

And then it happens. For some inexplicable reason, you feel as if a tour pro has jumped inside your body, grabbing that 5-iron and helping you hit a 170-yard beauty to the center of the green.

"Nice shot, Jimmy!"

"Great shot, partner!"

Now you're thinking that this game isn't so bad after all. *Hey, if I can hit that shot, I can hit any shot!*

It's a shot that everyone knows. It's the shot that brings you back.

The Backswing

The chances are pretty good that a little repair work on your setup will keep your scores down and your membership running. But the swing itself probably needs a little doctoring, too.

Do you know the first thing you should do to start your backswing? And I'm not talking about the trigger that starts it as we discussed in the previous chapter. I'm talking about after you pull the trigger. Then what do you do?

All the teaching pros throughout the formative years of golf, the guys and gals who helped pioneer the classic swing, claim that you must start the backswing with the hip turn.

Not the shoulders, not the arms, and certainly not the hands.

The hips start to turn, the arms naturally turn as the shoulders rotate; the wrists stay locked until the arms are about horizontal with the ground. You feel a stretching action as your left shoulder comes up under your chin, and you feel another stretch as your hips have reached the maximum coiling position.

At this point, the shoulders have out-turned the hips, and they should. In fact, many of today's top teachers believe that the ratio of shoulder turn to hip turn is crucial in storing power to release on the downswing.

The amount of hip turn today is clearly less than in past decades. It's even hard to find a teaching pro today who would encourage a full turn of the hips. Shoulders? Yes. Hips? No.

Never mind that Jones turned his hips as far as he turned his shoulders. In fact, watching his hips turn makes one wonder if this golfing genius was multi-jointed. So, today it's on golf's "What's Out" list. Yet years ago, Jones turned those hips to the tune of five major tournaments in his short amateur career. That enormous hip turn, incidentally, is what gave Jones his unmistakable swing.

At the top of the backswing, I like to feel four different conditions that assure me that what I've done so far is good.

(1) I feel the stretch not only in my shoulders but up my arms, all the way up to my hands, because I want my hands high. Is that important, you ask? Ask Raymond Floyd. Ask him how many tournaments he's won. He epitomizes the hands-high position at the top.

(2) I confirm a weight shift to the inside of my right foot that I know I can't hold very long because the sensation of forward power is overwhelming.

(3) I sense the status of my knees. What might be elementary to you has always been a problem for me, so I make it one of the four things I want to feel before I start my downswing. Specifically, I must feel that my right leg has not changed one iota from the setup position. Both knees were bent at setup; I want to know that they still are. The left knee kicks inward, of course, but **keeping both knees bent at the top of the backswing is crucial for producing a powerful, fluid swing.**

For many years, I had a tendency to straighten out the right knee as I completed the takeaway, and you can guess what else happened as I locked that knee. That's right. My head raised up, too.

(4) I check my grip at the top because it's at that point where many golfers do one of two things, either of which is not good. My tendency was always to tighten down on the grip, as if I were trying to strangle the club. The tension produced from such a glaring no-no can interrupt your timing and throw the whole swing out of kilter.

What's interesting about this finger-tightening flaw is a rather bizarre side effect. If you tighten up on your grip at the top of the swing as I used to, I can almost assure you that you also grit your teeth. A dentist I used to play with told me how common this problem is. He had a patient that clamped his teeth so tightly at the top of his backswing that he actually got severe headaches from playing golf. There are enough aspects of this game that can give you headaches. Don't add to them!

It's also interesting to note that golfers who hold their clubs properly at setup and on the way up to the top of the backswing will involuntarily tighten the grip at the moment of impact, as they should. You don't have to think about it. It just happens.

Now for that other mistake many players make at the top. Instead of maintaining the right grip pressure, they actually loosen the grip. A good teacher can detect this quickly because the clubhead will tend to drop just before the start of the downswing. I'm sure I don't have to list all the problems this can cause.

I can't forget a golf magazine article from years back that listed the top flaws among amateurs, as ranked by several tour players at the time. Although most of the answers were—as you would expect—lifting the head, a few named grip pressure as the chief culprit. A few others even mentioned lifting the left heel at the top. We need to talk about that.

The Left Heel:
To Lift Or Not To Lift

In the early '80s, a golf magazine featured a tip from a leading instructor that dealt primarily with the action at the top of the backswing. Of primary importance, and shown quite clearly in the illustration that accompanied the article, was the matter of lifting the left heel. The instructor said that raising the heel releases the power "stored in the coil," which was his reference phrase for the stretch developed in the shoulder turn. To further paraphrase this grand ol' teacher of golf, he said that you've just released all the energy you built up in a fine turn the moment the left heel comes up.

Well, during the time of that article, Johnny Miller and Jack Nicklaus were winning tournaments left and right and had become the stars of the tour. I'm sure I don't have to tell you that both Miller and Nicklaus raise their left heel, Miller in particular. In fact, Miller's foot work at the top and throughout the downswing had been the subject of discussion among the leading instructors at the time. If you watch old tapes of Miller during his earlier years, you can't help but wonder how this guy didn't twist an ankle or even fall over with such "unusual" footwork.

I doubt if he ever did hurt himself, but I do know that he made his mark on the tour with incredible drives off the tees. Same goes for Nicklaus. And many other pros, for that matter, who either lifted their left heel or rolled it over or twisted their feet as they unleased incredible power.

Today, you don't see many pros lifting their left heel. In fact, their footwork is rather boring to watch. What would seem to be a critical aspect of the basic swing would also seem to have become a standardized fundamental. It's clear that the new-school advice from those years took hold; it would seem as if pros who had started their training in those days, in modern form, and who have reached the tour today, were told to keep that heel down. Maybe a swishy two-step twist at the finish, but that's about all you see today that's worth noting.

Of course, Penick got into the act, too, claiming that he's an old-school teacher and liked to see the left heel come up. When Penick spoke, golfers listened. So another wave of tour pros began lifting the left heel.

Most instructors today will teach you either of two ways:

(1) Don't lift the left heel, or

(2) Don't worry about the left heel; let it do what feels right.

However, **no instructor today will let a student raise the left heel to such an extent that power and accuracy are clearly lost.** So maybe it's a matter of degree. A little's OK; a lot isn't. But don't tell Johnny Miller.

The Downswing

So, you're at the top... grip pressure is good, weight distribution seems right, hands are high, shoulders and hips are coiled, now what? **Those same legends of the game who we talked about earlier, who said to start the backswing with**

the hips, also said to start the downswing with the hips, too. In fact, it's one of Jones' most emphasized aspects of producing power.

Why? Because to start the hips first actually increases the stored energy in the coil... it increases the stretch between the arms and your body; you feel like a giant rubber band that's ready to snap!

Some of the old pros actually encouraged their students to try to further this stretch by consciously trying to hold back on the club as the hips turn to the target. Now, we don't want to get this stretching action to the point where you feel as if you're on a torturer's rack, but it's how power is produced. It's how golf balls are hit 300 yards. It's how baseballs are driven over the fence.

If you're tired of watching golf instruction videos, watch a baseball slugger in slow motion. As the hips begin to turn toward the ball, the arms "pull" the bat farther back with more shoulder turn, producing a striking amount of torque in the body. The hips not only are turning but sliding forward in what is called the "stride." The lower body moves one way while the upper body moves the opposite.

In both the golf and baseball worlds, I've found that few pros today actually talk about this action. It's as if it's a secret they don't want to reveal.

Unleashing The Power

As you come down with the club, you should feel as if your left arm is pulling the club down as your body releases torque. Snead was quite right when he said that you should feel it more in the last two fingers of your left hand. The reason for this is purely physiological. The tendons that control those fingers are the first to feel the stretch, so those two fingers actually do a considerable amount of the left hand's work in developing club speed. An involuntary action of tightening these fingers is natural.

It's interesting to note that the right hand doesn't contribute much until the moment when the wrists uncock. If you practice your swing, you'll feel these two specific instances of both power and increasing tightness in the fingers.

Most pros today teach golfers to delay the wrist action as long as possible so that you are reserving this added power until just before contact.

Where the upper body actions in the downswing usually come off as "natural" actions, the lower body's contribution to the shot is not at all a subconscious set of actions. In fact, it's where most average golfers lose power.

The knees, still flexed, should turn toward the target, helping to produce that recognizable "comma" shape at the instant of impact. As the hips continue turning, most long hitters will "slide" the hips slightly forward, further contributing to the comma shape. Nicklaus, Ernie Els, and Vijay Singh are masters of this subtle, yet highly effective, move.

Don't confuse it with a sway, as we discussed earlier. A sway, if you recall, is mostly from the upper body... most noticeable by the head sliding from the right side to the left. So let's get our terminology straight.

SLIDE: A slide (lower body) adds power without loss of accuracy.

SWAY: A sway (upper body) is a costly error particularly in terms of accuracy. It can cause your head to lead the shot, actually moving in front of the ball at impact. You must always keep your head behind the ball.

The Follow-Through

The follow-through completes the swing and is more important than most golfers think. Little regard is placed on the follow-through, and I can certainly attest to that as I paged through literally dozens of vintage books on golf.

Why? I don't have a clue. Unless it's because the shot is finished and the follow-through is deemed academic.

Arnold Palmer did not have a particularly pretty follow-through. In fact, there was less and less of one as he aged. But he still hit the ball in typical Arnie fashion. It's just another example of how top golfers can enjoy a long professional life with a little flaw here and a little flaw there. But I must tell you, I'm uncomfortable labeling any part of Arnie's game a "flaw." That's like telling Leonardo da Vinci that his "Mona Lisa" needed just a little more smile.

No. A golf swing should be judged by its result. And in Arnold's case, his swing made him the most recognizable and instrumental player in golf.

But as far as you and I are concerned, we better learn how to fully complete the swing. Amateurs do stupid things as a result of a forgotten follow-through.

"Bobby, you lifted up again."

How many times have you said this? How many times has it been said to you?

There are many reasons for it. A stance that's too erect. A hip slide that you aren't competent to make. Or the most common reason: being too anxious to see how well you hit the ball.

A good follow-though helps you stay down. A good follow-through works because it's part of the swing "program" that actually affects your swing *before* you hit the ball.

Subconsciously, you may let up on the downswing because you have programmed yourself to shorten the follow-through. Your faulty "program" may also cause you to push the shot, or worse... come over the top.

Whatever you do, follow through!

Tips & Tricks: Subtle Changes That Can Help Your Swing

Slow your takeaway:

It's good advice. After all, you're not hitting the ball on the backswing. But do you know how most average golfers react to this advice? They take the club back as if in slow-motion. By the time they get to the top, they forgot what course they're playing. Remember, *subtle* is the operative word. Take the club back a little slower, at least for the first third of the backswing. As Bob Uecker would say, "Ju-u-u-u-s-t a little slower.

Keep your takeaway low to the ground:

Don't lift the club up or yank it around. The way you bring the club up sets the program for the way you take it down. A smooth takeaway is conducive to a fluid swing. The operative word here is *smooth*. Or is it?

A pro I talk to from time to time from another club says he's had many a hard time explaining exactly what a low takeaway feels like. "I was about ready to give up on this one member," he told me. "She just didn't get the idea of a nice smooth takeaway until I told her to 'sweep' the club back. Now I use that word over and over. Sweep! Sweep the club back!"

Let your wrists cock naturally:

As you swing the club back, your wrists will bend your hands naturally, in a position that holds the club vertically. For most golfers, this generally happens when the club is parallel to the ground, but it depends on the grip and the stature of the player.

Years ago, this position was given a name and a series of articles written about it in nearly every golf magazine. It was called the "L" configuration (or L-Swing), as if your arms are the bottom of the "L" and your club is the ascender part of the letter.

There are a couple of solid pluses to this tip:

(1) The holding stress of the club is greatly diminished at this point in your swing. It's obviously easier to hold a club upright than to hold it out at an angle.

(2) This position encourages a greater arc and may actually make it easier to take the club to full parallel at the top.

What many of the instructors promoting this concept missed, in my opinion, was making it clear that the wrist-cocking action is a gradual one, beginning almost instantly with the takeaway. Some golfers would actually take the club back without any wrist action and then abruptly break the wrist when the club reached parallel position with the ground. It's a wonder that some golfers didn't *literally* break their wrists with this misinterpretation.

The tip clashed with the widely held advice of the old pros who recommended that the wrists remain locked through the takeaway and then naturally begin to unlock at about the same parallel position where the L-Swing would have the wrists already cocked.

Nicklaus follows the old-school method and does not begin to unlock his wrists until the club is about parallel. His swing chart at

this position shows an incredible extension of the club and the appearance of great power building. In contrast, Corey Pavin likes the L-Swing, as do several other pros who joined the tour during that same stretch of years. Pavin's swing, as you would guess, appears more compact, and there's obviously less wrist action at the top, which tends to get the club into the same ideal position from swing to swing.

The sensible advice here, since there is clearly no consensus, is to try both ways and see which one works best for you. Personally, I much prefer the old-school method of keeping your wrists locked through the takeaway and start the cocking action where it comes naturally.

An interesting sidebar to this discussion involves an old playing partner of mine who put his own twist on where the wrists break. His way: He never broke his wrists! He brought the club up smoothly and in a nice radius as he should, but he forgot to unlock his wrists. At the top of his backswing, the club was standing straight up in the air! He said it helped him get a full shoulder turn. Of course it would. He was right about that. But he was losing power by not being able to use his wrists on the downswing!

Trying to hit a golf ball without cocking your wrists is like trying to shoot a gun without pulling the hammer back! Hey, to each his own, right? I should tell you, though... of all the matches we played, he beat me more times than I want to remember!

Don't pause at the top:

Most high-handicap golfers will say that they do not pause at the top. Most of these golfers would be wrong. When a golf instructor tells you not to pause at the top, the common reaction from the student is, "I don't." But they do. And it's a big contributor to over-the-top swings that send your shots slicing. And that pause that you don't think you make can break the flow of a nice fluid swing.

There are so many things happening at the top, or let's say, that *should* be happening, clearly indicating that no work stoppage is going on.

For one, the pros tend to push off from their right foot *before* the club has reached its full extension. In a sense, this action starts the hips turning and the lower body sliding into the shot, developing the stretch that you feel all the way up to your hands. Remember? And it's the start of this lower body action *before* the club has changed direction that makes the top of the swing an integral part of *continuous* action.

CHAPTER 4
Off The Tee

"I walked over to the tee and saw this new kid from West Virginia (Sam Snead) hit his drive. I not only saw it, I heard it. It sounded like a rifle and the ball flew like a bullet. I knew right that moment that my future was not as a tour player."

—*Harvey Penick*

Most of you are familiar with the now trite expression coined by Sam Snead, "You drive for show and putt for dough."

Do we really want to challenge that time-tested doctrine of golf? Well, yes, we do. Sam's famous words seem to suggest that a long drive, I mean a *really* long drive, will bring out the applause from the gallery, but tournaments are won on the greens. Birdie putts don't have to be center-cup. They don't have to be pretty. They don't even have to be long. They just have to drop.

I guess Sam didn't care whether or not the gallery around the greens enjoyed watching him tap in for birdie. He enjoyed it all the way to the bank.

But the key question is, how did he get to the green? How did he put himself in position to make birdie? Read on.

Play Your Shot In Anticipation Of The *Next* Shot

It's tough to argue, but here's the truth about golf shots that you probably already know, but just never really thought about. **Every shot, up to that last putt, is geared to one thing: the next shot.** It's no different from a billiard player's strategy. The idea is to make a ball *and* leave the cue ball in perfect position for the next shot.

Whenever players tell me that they can't get off the tee well, I know that they will be fighting the course with tough shots all the way to the green. Even a long drive isn't enough. It has to find the fairway. And, specifically, the *right* part of the fairway that will make the approach shot easier.

Never, ever, underestimate the importance of a straight drive, even if you aren't out as far as your playing buddies.

As you work on your drives, your first concern must be accuracy. That's right. First, work on hitting a straight ball. Distance, as important as that is, is second on the list.

I could quote dozens of top pros from days past and days present who would tell you that long, uncontrolled drives rarely win the marbles. A long drive into the rough will most often end up behind another drive that's shorter but *in the fairway*. Your ball will run farther in the short grass; it will probably stop within a few feet in heavier rough.

But wait! There's more! That same shorter drive in the fairway will usually outperform a long drive burdened with a slice or hook. You've heard it a hundred times: **When the ball makes an unwanted turn, it loses distance, not to mention accuracy.**

If you must choose one or the other at this stage in your game, it's an easy decision. Take accuracy over distance every time.

In a later chapter on playing with physical ailments and handicaps, it will become quite clear that in order to play a competitive round while fighting health problems, you must first get off the tee with a straight ball.

It's also true as age catches up with you. Or is it the other way around? Regardless. A straight drive almost always keeps you in the game.

Here are several subtle changes you can make to help ensure an accurate drive.

Tips & Tricks:
Subtle Changes That Can Help Your Accuracy Off The Tees

Learn how to hit the ball on the sweet spot:

Easier said than done, but the difference between a solid "on the spot" hit and a strike off the toe or heel is more than a distance loss… it's what a club designer I know calls an "anybody's guess" shot… anybody's guess where that ball is going to end up.

Over the years, club designers have concocted certain design parameters, particularly for woods and metal woods, that are supposed to correct for off-center hits.

1. Horizontal face bulge is one of those designs purported to help the ball spin in an opposing direction to the contour of the face. If you strike the ball on the toe, the theory to the design is that the ball will spin to the left to help bring the ball back into the fairway. Hah!

2. Vertical face roll is a design that is particularly annoying to the upper echelon of golfers who, frankly, don't need it. It causes more pop-ups and "worm-burners," as we all like to call them, than if the clubface's vertical roll were flattened down to its advertised loft angle.

3. Face progression is another tricky design that takes into account the moment of impact. Several years ago, a leading club manufacturer came out with a line of metal woods and irons with significant off-set (negative progression) that meant you would strike the ball about half an inch later than you expected to. You'll gain more loft, certainly, but why not just build the loft into the club's natural loft angle? Why not? Because then a 7-iron might be really an 8-iron.

Normal progression can result in the opposite effect: what you think is a 7-iron is really a 6-iron. No wonder you were hitting that new 7-iron farther than your old 7-iron. Watch out for these tricky ploys from club manufacturers.

All of these "tricks of the trade" can make it difficult for the average golfer to find the sweet spot on that trusty ol' 3-wood, or any club for that matter, including a putter. It's easy to find the sweet spot. Here's how:

How to find the sweet spot:

Simply hold the club at or near the grip so that the club is hanging in the position where you would strike the ball. That is, with the sole parallel to the ground. Yes, you'll have to cock the club outward somewhat with your hand holding the grip. Next, with your other hand, tap on the clubface (I prefer to do this with my first knuckle) and see how the clubhead responds. If you strike the sweet spot, the club will move smoothly backward. In any other spot, the club will torque (rotate) and may actually vibrate. You can feel the turning or vibrating action in your hand holding the club. But the evidence is clear; the action of the clubface will be a surprise to any golfer who never performed this simple test.

Incidentally, that sweet spot you found is a point; it's not a spot. And certainly not an "area." **So when you hear a club manufacturer's claim on TV that its new driver has an "enlarged" or "extended" sweet spot, you'll know that it's time to put the boots on.** As I said earlier, there are a few things a club designer can do to improve performance on off-center hits, but a club designer cannot make the sweet spot bigger.

Some golfers refer to the sweet spot as the "center of gravity," which has become an accepted term for this elusive spot. But even that term is wrong since we're talking about a three-dimensional object. The actual center of gravity would be somewhere inside the clubhead!

The point on the clubface that you've found through our little test described above is really the "center of percussion." And it would be more appropriate in a discussion of striking tools such as a hammer, where the center of percussion would be... take a guess... yes, in the handle.

Hand-and-eye coordination:

OK, so now you know where your sweet spot is, even though I have now thoroughly confused you, but how do you hit that spot—whatever you want to call it—every time? I hate the answer to this question but it's the only answer there is! Practice your hand-eye coordination!

I base my contempt on this simplistic answer because, in high school, I was never one who could hit a jump-shot from 20 feet out, but I was "Mr. Reliable" shooting layups. Unfortunately, my layup acumen didn't get me on the team. In football, I could throw a nice, tight, spiral but I never came close to the intended receiver. I think the cheerleaders caught more of my passes than the guys running down the sidelines. Baseball? I wanted to pitch but no one wanted to stand in the batter's box. There were just too many injuries.

The only tips I can give you... and you must take into account who's giving these tips... is to always keep your eye on the object you are going to catch, hit, or throw to. Since we can't really throw a golf ball (except in those rare times when you're in a deep trap and your partner isn't looking), and we obviously don't want to catch a golf ball, that leaves hitting the golf ball as the one we want to work on.

The consensus among long drivers is to always, always keep your eye on the ball. How many times have we heard that one? And no matter how well you keep your eye on the ball, locking in the target, if you move your head or veer left or right, you'll miss the target. We're not flying F-16s here with sophisticated target lock-in software. We're humans who have to train ourselves to compensate for unexpected body movements as we lunge for the ball. And, surprisingly, our own computers can do this.

To believe it, all you have to do is watch a trick-shot artist who can hit a golf ball tossed into the air like a baseball while standing on a wobbly chair, or resting on his knees. Unbelievably, these masters of hand-eye coordination—while fettered in chains, with one arm tied behind the back, and blindfolded—can even hit a drive you'd give your first born for!

Seriously. Go to a PGA Tour event. Most all tournaments today feature these acrobats of golf as part of the activities during the pro-am schedule. It will give you all the impetus you need to practice hand-eye coordination.

There are several ways to practice. My favorite is one you can do at home... simply bouncing a golf ball on the face of a wedge. See if you can do it 20 times without missing. A word of caution: Don't try this drill with a 2-iron. And don't do it anywhere near your wife's collection of antique glass slippers.

Another practice routine is worth mentioning: Get on the range and practice your drives with just your left arm. And try this one: Grip way down on a 60-degree wedge and practice with a half-swing. You should tee the ball, though, and not worry about hitting down on the ball. The idea here is to shorten the arc.

Last on the list is perhaps the best of all: Get yourself three golf balls. Start with two and juggle them. Then, once you've got the hang of it, add the third ball. Can you think of any better example of hand-eye coordination than juggling?

Obviously, hand-eye coordination is important in all sports, but golf in particular. Think, for a moment, how just the slightest improper body movement could otherwise throw you off a mere fraction of an inch. The right knee straightens, the head comes up, the body sways, the right shoulder drops... the list is endless. To produce a perfect golf swing is quite an achievement, when you think about it. You have to "juggle" fifty things to remember, and make instant compensations, all within 1.28 seconds!

I shouldn't make light of the importance of good hand-eye coordination, but I'll never forget what a famous golf instructor had to say about his preference for students whom he would rather teach. His preference: athletes. He went on and on about how much easier it is to teach a hockey player, baseball player, football quarterback or receiver, or even a basketball player. "They all have great hand-eye coordination," he said.

Hmm. For those of you who enjoy celebrity pro-ams, who could forget a particular pro basketball player, a master on the court... a disaster on the fairways. Can you say, "Charles Barkley"?

Keep It Simple:

Accuracy comes from a rather simplistic execution of the proper golf swing: turn to the top, turn again to start the swing, shift weight, and slide lower body (don't sway). The more you practice the proper swing, the more programmed it becomes and the fewer things you have to think about. And that's the key here. There's so much thinking going on for the average golfer that something as important as hand-eye coordination gets left in the discard pile.

And there's something else you should know when we talk about programming a swing. You see, **most of the concentration that's done is during the setup. Good golfers, even the top pros, are thinking through the movements culminating with the strike of the golf ball zinging its way to the target. It's a golfer's pre-flight checklist and nothing dare be missed.**

Why? Because at the instant the swing begins, there is little time to think about anything. And from the top of the swing onward, there is no time at all. The swing is finished in a matter of nanoseconds. **Top golfers have developed—and learned to trust—their programmed swing.**

When a golfer is concentrating during setup, it is merely a playback of the program. When you are comfortable that the program has not been corrupted, you're cleared for takeoff.

Rhythm, who could ask for anything more:

It's absolutely true. If you watch a pro golfer with a less than admirable swing, don't think for a moment that this particular golfer is lacking rhythm. There's a distinct rhythm to that swing that might be hard to notice at first, but it's there. Otherwise, *he* wouldn't be there.

Demaret, Sarazen, and particularly Byron Nelson preached the importance of developing a rhythm to the swing. Most average golfers today have a certain rhythm up to the top, but it's there that things can begin to go wrong. So, a special drill was developed years ago to help golfers feel the right side moving smoothly into the shot.

It involved a simple half-swing with a 7-iron. The idea was to swing the club at about 70 percent power, but only up to the point where the club is parallel with the ground. The shortened downswing would end with an interrupted follow-through just at the point before you would naturally come up with your head. The left elbow remained locked during this drill. Even with this compromise in upper-body action, it made it easier to work on the lower body, particularly the weight shift, knee, and foot action.

After a golfer felt the rhythm, the balance of the drill was to continuously repeat it, taking the club up in a half-swing, and then down but only partially through as noted above, then immediately back up, and through, up and through.

The drill is one of my favorites. It helps to improve accuracy by smoothing out the more complicated motions of the full swing. Try it.

As a fringe benefit, you'll also learn how to build power by feeling it gather steam from your right side as you shift your weight from the inside of your right foot to the left foot while sliding the lower body toward the target. Through continuous up-and-through action of the "second half" of the swing, you'll quickly adjust to the full swing and retain the new rhythm you've just acquired.

"Steady as she goes":

An old pro used to say this time and time again when with a student on the practice tees. Another of his favorite lines was, "You're listing to the right." The metaphor is indeed appropriate for golfers, particularly those who have a problem with balance. If you fall back on your heels at the top of the swing, or "list" to the right as you complete the downswing, what chance do you have of hitting a solid golf shot?

Just as a ship needs to have the weight of its cargo balanced in the hold, a golfer needs to feel balanced, too, and keep that feeling of balance throughout the swing. Sure, at the top there's an unbalanced feeling of weight on the inside right wanting to shift over to the full left... we know that... but I was talking about backward and forward weight balance.

Try to keep your majority weight centered on the balls of your feet, as we've talked about before in the chapter on setup. There seems to be no consensus among the old pros for the exact distribution of weight; several times I noted that a full and uniform distribution of weight from heel to toe was recommended. Whatever. Go with what feels the most balanced for you. The key here is to feel both balanced and firm in your stance so that you can fully support and stabilize yourself throughout the swing.

Having said that, I'm reminded of a quick story.

One of my favorite golf partners, whom I dearly miss, almost always fell forward as he completed his powerful swing. I wanted to help him; I knew what was wrong, but I didn't dare. "Go talk to one of the pros, Jack, and get that fixed," I pleaded. "You'll hit the ball a mile farther."

But like so many golfers today, Jack wanted to fix it himself. I guess it's a "man thing." We nicknamed him "Tool Man" because if he wasn't under the hood he was under the sink. With all due respect to Tim Taylor, there are some things you need to have an expert look into.

I can't forget the day that Jack wound up a swing so tightly on a long par-5 that he fell forward unleashing it, getting tangled up with his club, and falling square on his face. "I'm OK," he said. Never mind the bloodied nose. He looked like he had just gone six rounds with Mike Tyson. And we did find his ball. About half a mile down the road that runs along the *right* side of the fairway.

Anyhow, I had always believed that Jack's swing plane was too steep, and that, coupled with his muscular upper-body weight, would tend to shift him forward and throw his club out over the target line. I always knew before he started his downswing if he was going to hit a good shot or not. It was easy. I'd just look at his feet. If he was on his tippy toes, he was in trouble.

So be aware of steep swing planes. It's a problem especially for guys with large, well-defined, upper-bodies. It's just easier for them to swing more upright, I guess. There's less in the way. And

I suppose it's also true for women golfers who have a well-defined... uh, well, you know.

To check your swing plane, some instructors recommend simply noting the position of your hands at the top of the backswing. It's arguable as to the reference to use, but most agree that simply experimenting with different swing planes should help immensely.

As important as this aspect of the swing is to accuracy, I'm not comfortable letting the subject rest by simply telling you that pros, young and old, have such a wide disparity among their recommendations. So let's stay with it a moment.

A steep swing plane generally doesn't allow for a good shoulder turn. You should be able to readily detect that telltale sign. With a proper plane to swing on, you'll feel the shoulder action working correctly, and you'll feel as if your hands are behind you, not beside you, and certainly not in front of you. If they are in front of you, an outside-in (over the top) swing—the chief cause of a slice—is all but guaranteed.

Just remember that with the proper swing plane, you are virtually forced to hit the ball from the inside out.

Don't try to steer the club along the target line:

I talk about curing a slice in more than one section of this book because there are many factors that can contribute to it. But what you have just read is perhaps the most condemned of all faults: a chief contributor to that nasty outside-in swing.

Amateurs often try to steer the ball off the tee, right down the target line, and sometimes they even try to lift the ball into the air by lifting up instead of staying down and letting the club naturally elevate the ball. On the tee, we want to have the picture of hitting *through* the ball. When hitting an approach shot, or a tee-shot to a par 3 green, we might want to hit *down* on the ball to impart backspin. We'll talk about that in more detail in the next chapter on approach shots. But, for now, let's get back to that matter of trying to steer the golf ball.

If a golfer tries to shape the downswing to line up with and follow the target line, it will probably result in a sliced tee-shot because the club did not "join" the target line from the inside. It probably swept over the line and joined it from the outside.

Decades ago, instructors used a popular method to convince golfers that they should not try to line up the downswing with the target line.

It was hard for beginning golfers to believe and even weekend golfers were in doubt as to the wisdom of this advice. By now I'm sure you can figure out for yourself why trying to get the club on the target line almost always results in an outside-in swing. This fixation that many golfers have about that target line probably explains why so many golfers slice in the first place.

Here's the way the instructors fixed the problem:

They would tell their students to strike the ball as if they were aiming out to the right of the target line. In a sense, the idea is to follow the natural direction of the swing, which, if you think about it, is not at all along the target line but at an angle to it.

"I can't do that," a golfer would complain. "I'd be hitting the ball to the right of my target!"

"Go ahead and try it," the teacher would insist.

And where did the ball go? Why, straight down the middle.

It only *seemed* as if the ball were hit off-target. It only *seemed* as if the ball should go to the right.

Of course, you don't want to exaggerate this tip. By throwing away some essential fundamentals, you could actually hit the ball to the right. Keep the basics you've learned intact, such as brushing your upper left arm across your chest on both the backswing and downswing and keeping a keen eye on your swing plane.

Left shoulder under chin, but what is your right shoulder doing?

At the top of the swing, you know your left shoulder belongs under your chin. And you know that your right shoulder is behind you, confirming the coil of power you've just created. But what happens to that right shoulder as you start your downswing is crucial to hitting a straight ball.

A slicer should be able to feel the right shoulder move forward, changing the direction of attack for the hands. You know the routine by now: The hands are pushed out and moving inward instead of staying inward and moving out.

The fix is a simple one. And, once again, it requires a mental thought that must eventually become part of your involuntary swing program. Think of your right shoulder as moving straight down. It should not be pulled outward by your hands moving forward (toward the target line) but instead should simply *drop* into the swing, which, in effect, helps to keep your hands inside.

So, have we cured the slice? Are you now able to hit a straight ball? It seems as if there are too many things to be concerned about, but it isn't really that many at all. With time, as I said earlier, all of these "fixin's" will become a part of your natural swing. Enjoy it. You've earned it. Now you can start working on your partner's game. He'll love you for it.

Accuracy And Length

We really have to put some measurements on these important, "accurate" drives we've been talking about. Sure, it's a big plus to know that you can almost always hit your ball onto the fairway, landing in a safe area for your next shot. But how far, would you say, is minimally acceptable to still shoot a good round?

It's a fair question, and I'm sure the flood of answers I'd get would depend on age and physical condition, the number of rounds you play, and, well, you know, whether you typically break 80 or 100.

Maybe there isn't a "minimally acceptable" length because of all these variables, but I think there should be. If you plop your drive out there nice and straight, but only hit it 120 yards, that won't bring home the bacon. You might as well drive with your 8- or 9-iron.

You'll certainly enjoy the game more, and shoot far better scores, if you can at least hit the ball 200 yards on the fly. That's *on the fly*. Here's why I say that.

Most course designers today determine a landing area of from 200 to 275 yards from the middle tees. It's getting longer as the years go by because of improvements to the ball and the equipment. No big surprise, of course, but it can be a big frustration if you can't reach that 200 yards to clear a lake, heather, sand, a stream, or just an intentional "fault" in the fairway designed to "collect" your drive, literally stopping it in its tracks.

Golf courses today are becoming player *un*-friendly, and many golfers looking for a nice club to join are not interested in playing on championship courses that severely test your skills... and your resolve. "Who needs it?" you'll hear often, from golfers who are not that bad, but not that long off the tee.

Yeah, I know, you can always make up for these tough courses by playing the easier tees. Well, I don't know about you but I know that I certainly don't want to walk up to the tee box that's right in front of the women's tees. No thanks. Even if I'm playing with older players, I encourage them to at least try the white tees (our tee boxes are coded black, blue, white, gold, and red). And you know what, more often than not they played well and scored nearly the same as from the shorter tees that they usually play.

Let me put it bluntly. If you have to move down to the short tees to enjoy your course, you need to find another course.

At my club, the first hole is a brutal test of both accuracy and distance. It's a par-5 with a wide ravine that runs across the fairway right in front of the tee box. To clear the ravine, you need 210 yards on the fly from the white tees. The shorter tees are positioned to the side of the ravine, more or less, so you really don't have to worry about it much. The short tees take most of it out of play. And, as most members would say, those short tees take the teeth out of the hole.

No one likes to have their challenges taken away. After all, golf *is* a challenge. **Play from the tees that challenge you.** In other words, play the course tough... don't sucker-punch it to beat it. Where's the satisfaction in that?

Many years ago, I was fortunate to be able to play Pine Valley. It's generally regarded as the toughest test of golf. In fact, the best way to describe it is to quote Babe Ruth: "Hell, finding the greens isn't the problem. I can't find the fairways!" Obviously, he had a rough time with it. (Pardon the pun.)

I can understand. That first hole at my club that I told you about is a good example of what you'll find at Pine Valley. Just multiply that hole by 18!

As important as accuracy is, short tee-shots on that wicked course would mean a long day.

So let's work on lengthening our drives. Not because you have a round scheduled at Pine Valley, but because every golf course will be easier for you to play if you can get off the tees. Here are a few words of wisdom from golfers who play from the championship tees. You may not get there, but I'll bet you'll get close.

Tips & Tricks:
Subtle Changes That Can Help Your Distance Off The Tees

Right foot as a backstop:

I love this one. It's a "feeling" tip that seems to work for everyone. When you're at the top of your backswing and ready to start the hips turning, you're also in position to start the weight shift with a sliding action that we've already talked about. The lower body "slides" to the left, knees jut toward the target, and those turning hips pull the arms down with incredible force. For that instant at the top, with your weight on the inside of the right foot, push off with your right foot as you start the lower body actions.

Some golfers today still do what the old-timers used to do: they push down into the soil with the inside of their right shoe, as if forming a trench to give them a better push-off. Although the USGA has ruled in a similar case that such an action is "improving your stance," I'm telling you this so that you can get a better picture as to how the right foot can help you gain power.

The right stance for distance:

Instructional books on golf spend considerable time on two things: the grip and foot position in the setup. The importance of having the right grip (for *you*) is obvious, but feet position is clearly not a consensus. Many of these golf books look more like dance books. Are we hitting a golf ball or doing the Bossa Nova?

Dropping the right foot back a few inches is an old trick that is supposed to help you cure a slice. But most teachers, then and now, would rather see a golfer tee it up with the feet equidistant from the target line and positioned so that the toes are pointing outward, perhaps 10 to 15 degrees.*

---

*This simple, yet effective stance assumes that the golfer is not trying to work the ball, a subject we'll discuss in the next chapter.

There's little talk anymore about whether or not you want an open or closed stance. Just place your feet at shoulder width, maybe a little more if you're stocky, a little less if you're tall, bend those knees and keep that right knee bent throughout the swing. I mention the knees because an improper stance can affect the way they perform. And they do perform.

What can happen when weekend golfers experiment with different feet configurations is rarely advantageous. In some positions, the knees will not bend properly, or they might not freely "slide" toward the target on the downswing.

And there are other problems to deal with. Balance could be difficult to hold, your turn could be restricted, the weight shift might feel awkward, and, perhaps worst of all, the clubface might not square itself at impact.

Long drives come from a solid foundation. If your stance is unusual, it might be holding you back.

Follow through for added distance:

It's hard to convince an average golfer that a proper follow-through can actually improve your distance. But it's true. We talked about it in the previous chapter. Now let's talk about it again in detail.

Although the follow-through happens *after* the ball is launched, the program you develop over years and years of swinging a golf club will tend to be affected as a whole by any singular event during the swing, before or after you strike the ball. **The most typical result of a poor follow-through is the involuntary tendency to want to slow down the swing at impact as if it's some sort of pre-preparation for the abrupt stop you are about to make.**

I use the term "involuntary" because the premature slowdown happens even though the player doesn't want it to. Still, golfers allow it to happen time and time again. Why? Because it's been ingrained into their programs.

Here's the right way to follow through when you're on the tee.

Ideally, the wrists will relock after impact and stay locked for a good 90 degrees of follow-through. In fact, both the left and right arms stay straight (no elbow bend) right up to that same 90-degree position. It's only after this position is reached that the head comes up with the body; the weight, remarkably, remains on the left foot, and the right heel naturally raises to accommodate the weight shift to the left side.

As you would expect, there are only a few players on any of the major tours today who don't have a solid follow-through. I'm willing to bet that most of them are on the Champions Tour because a picture-perfect follow-through can be physically tough to pull off, shot after shot. It's easier, obviously, to relax a little earlier.

But it can be costly.

The right arm does not "go along for the ride":

You hear it all the time. "The right arm just goes along for the ride." Cases are cited of one-armed golfers who can drive the ball 300 yards with just their left arm. Even better golfers believe that the power is in the left arm. Well, there's power in the left arm, all right, but there's power in the right arm, too. In fact, over 90 percent of your major muscles are involved in the golf swing. It's not just one arm or the other, or one leg or the other. It's the entire body moving in harmony as one unit.

But as far as the right arm is concerned, it has a lot going for it to produce power. And you can see it best if you visualize just the right arm during the downswing. Unlike the left arm, the elbow of the right arm releases as the wrists uncock for a dual source of hammering power. In addition, a fulcrum-like action is produced by the position-ing of the elbow during the last third of the down-swing, giving the right forearm a quasi-lever source of power, even though the arm is freely moving.

Never underestimate the contribution your right arm makes to a powerful golf swing. **Several golfers today, including Jim Thorpe and Allen Doyle of the Champions Tour have an abbre-viated backswing, choosing instead to focus their power in the last third of the golf swing (the impact zone). It's not only where stored power is released, but where new power is generated.**

And guess what? The right arm is the key component.

CHAPTER 5

The Approach Shot

A competitor once said this about
Ben Hogan, widely regarded as one of
the shrewdest players: "He can play
better than most players because he
can think better than most players."

I live in Michigan, which means that if I want
to play golf during the winter months, I have to
fly somewhere. Preferably, where the sun is actually visible... and warm. Florida and California are
where I usually head. For other golfers in this
Winter Wonderland (hah!) who, for whatever reason, can't escape the winter (too busy at work is
the common excuse, "I just can't get away"), the
only chance you'll have to get your fix on golf is to
watch it on TV. Now, I don't know about you,
but I subscribe to the "sex theory" of watching golf

on TV. That's right. I'd rather be doing it than watching someone else doing it.

Watching guys play golf on TV, especially in Hawaii, only exacerbates the problem for me. OK. Watching golf tournaments on TV helps, but a better way to enjoy the tournament is to actually be there. That's why I like to set up my golf vacations when a PGA event is scheduled nearby.

For those of you who have never walked the ropes at a golf tournament, let me tell you what you can learn from doing this. By simply watching pros *inside* the ropes, you can help your game. But I think there's an optimum way to get the most out of your experience.

If you position yourself behind a tee and watch a few 300-yard drives zip down the fairway, you'll be impressed for all of about 20 minutes. Two or three groups go off, you watch the tee-shots, and you find yourself humming the words to Peggy Lee's "Is That All There is?" I hate to say this, but after you've seen a dozen or so drives that all seem to land in the exact same spot, you want to get up and move. And you should. Because that's not where you'll see real evidence that these guys are pros.

No. Long drives are not going to impress you after the first few oohs and ahs. There are guys at our club, at *any* club, who can hit it as far. So what's the big deal?!

Here's what you do instead:

Start walking to that spot where all the drives landed. That's where you want to position yourself, assuming it's a par-4 hole, because the next shots are the shots that count. And you'll be ooh-ing and ah-ing all over the place. You won't believe how accurate these guys are with their second shots—the approach shots—until you watch them in person. **You'll quickly see why pros make so many birdies. Because they set themselves up for short putts with great approach shots!**

I don't care if their tee-shots went a little astray. And it would seem, sometimes, as if it doesn't make that much difference to the pros, either. Second shots from a fairway trap, a downhill lie, an uphill lie, a sidehill lie, a few lousy trees in their way... it just doesn't seem to make any difference. They zero in on the pin and take everything else, including those trees, out of play. Average golfers call it a recovery shot. But for the pros, the shot is merely routine.

I suppose you could position yourself around a green and watch these magnificent approach shots land, like 747s stacked up at O'Hare. And it is impressive, indeed. By watching from the green, you can then watch them make those birdie putts. But I rank that right up there with watching tee-shots fly. A few putts made and I'm bored again.

The next time you have an opportunity to watch a PGA event, take my advice and stand just a few feet back from the spot where the golfers are hitting their approach shots. Always try to position yourself so that the sun is behind you (on your side of the fairway). That way, you can watch the pros' tee-shots come in and then easily follow their second shots to the green.

What you'll take from the experience is an important lesson in golf. I'm willing to bet that you'll be anxious to get to the practice range and hit your low- and mid-irons. Or fairway woods, if that's your speed. Pick a spot out on the range and see how close you can come.

Remember, the approach shot is the most important shot in golf. It puts you in position to make birdie.

Straight To The Pin!

Lloyd Mangrum used to tell his students to always shoot for the green. In a later quote, he changed it a little and said "… shoot for the pin."

Well, duh! What did he expect golfers to do, shoot for the traps?!

The fact is, Mangrum was making a most important point in such a simplistic way because he hoped his students would always remember the advice.

What he was referring to was the tendency—then and today—for weekend golfers to try to "shape" their shots to fall on the green... with a little luck. Of course, most weekend golfers already have a "shape" to their shots. They just compensate for it by aiming a little left or right.

Do you fade the ball? Then you probably play your fade. You would, of course, aim a little left of the target and work the ball to the pin. A player who draws the ball would aim a little right of the target and hope that the ball comes in on the runway.

Mangrum clearly did not like the idea of compensating in the direction of aim. His advice was to learn how to hit a straight ball. And who could argue?

We all know there are obvious exceptions when we need to hit a fade or a draw:

(1) when working the ball around a tree that has no business being there in the first place,

(2) bending the ball around a dogleg, or

(3) simply playing the wind.

But this isn't what Mangrum was talking about. He was plainly concerned about players who could only hit one type of shot... slices, hooks, fades, draws, whatever... any shot other than a straight shot.

He couldn't understand why players would resign themselves to this handicap and not spend more time on the range learning how to hit a straight ball. He called it a "flaw" that too many golfers accept. "You'll never fix the flaw if you always play for it," he said.

This advice from decades ago was brought back to the forefront while I watched a major Champions Tour tournament on television recently. On a short par-5 (short for the pros), a player was faced with a tough second shot to the green, a green that did not open to the fairway, but was sitting rather cockeyed with the front pointed more to the left. The long, narrow green bordered a nasty water hazard all along the left side. The right side was protected with a large bunker in front. The pin was at the back of the green about 20 feet behind the bunker.

It was ill-advised for players to hit to the left side of the fairway to be in the best position they could for their second shots to the green. Why? More water, strategically placed about where a good tee-shot would drop.

All three tee-shots, as I recall, were hit safely to the right center of the fairway, about 200 yards from the green. One of the announcers in the booth said that the players should hit a fade, aiming toward the water and then bringing the ball back in, lining up with the long axis of the green. And that's exactly how the first player set up the shot. The only problem was, the ball didn't fade enough and ended up hanging on the bank just inches from the water.

The next player in the group took aim in exactly the same way. His fade worked, but the ball fell short of the green. The TV announcer chastised him for being too conservative. "Yeah, I think he was afraid of the water," said the other announcer.

The third member of the group decided to play the shot a little differently. He set up his shot straight to the pin. The announcer in the booth was excited: "He's going for the pin, I'd say. I hope he clears the bunker or he can figure on bogey at best... the way the green slopes away toward the back, that would be a tough sand shot."

The smartest player of the group took dead aim for the pin, popped it up high and straight, dropping the ball five feet behind the cup. It spun back to within two feet for an easy putt.

The Eagle had landed.

Hitting A Fairway Wood

If you're always uptight about hitting a 3-wood from the fairway or light rough because you can't tee it up, that's a strong indicator that you're playing the fairway shot incorrectly. You're playing it as if you're on the tee. And if you do play from the fairway the same way you play from the tee, chances are, you top the ball more often than not. Am I right?

On the tee, you want to hit the ball at the exact bottom of the downswing, or slightly on the upswing in some cases, in order to gain distance by putting the proper spin on the ball. Everyone likes to see a ball land and roll seemingly forever. But you don't want to aim for the green with a shot like that, do you? What's the point of having the ball land on the green and roll off the back? I'm rushing to talk about spin control here in the hope that you can figure out your own problem with those fairway woods.

Sure. You've got it now. You're not hitting down on the ball. I'm sure you've heard it time and time again. But you're just not doing it. Why? Well, you're not alone. A lot of golfers are uptight about hitting that kind of shot, too. They're afraid they're going to stick the wood in the ground behind the ball or bounce the club off the ground and into the ball. I'm not sure which is worse.

Some golfers are afraid they're going to pop the ball up, or even afraid that by hitting down, the ball won't *go* up!

There was this guy I once played with who always used irons in the fairway... never a wood, because he was afraid he would break the club! He had no swing with the woods, really. He just picked up the club and slammed it down. But put a 5-iron in his hands and he'd sweep it back smooth and easy, a nice turn, a little shift, and he'd spank that ball on the downswing. Boy, is this game mental, or what?

Hitting down on the ball doesn't mean you want to drive it into the ground! It simply means hitting the ball just before the bottom of the downswing... while the club is still on its downward path. The natural loft of the club will send the ball into the air. You hit down; the ball goes up. You simply have to trust the club.

Most of the old pros were rather simple in their instruction on hitting from the fairway. To ensure a downward blow, they taught their students to keep the same swing and the same setup except for one minor adjustment: Instead of playing the ball off the inside of the left foot, simply move forward (toward the target) a few inches and play the ball closer to the center of your stance.

It's important that you know exactly where the bottom of your swing is in relation to your stance. That way you'll know exactly where to position the ball relative to your feet. Always take a few practice swings to get a good feel for what the old pros used to call "the bottom of the trench." Remember, you'll want to strike the ball a little earlier in your swing, so position yourself accordingly.

Snead made a point of telling his students not to do anything special with the fairway wood, other than ball positioning. Just a natural swing. But few, apparently, listened. Here's his list of all the "don'ts" that you don't want to do:

Don't pick up the club
Don't drop your right shoulder
Don't drop your hands
Don't stoop; don't scoop
Don't lunge at it

All of these things you wouldn't do on the tee, would you? So, why do them in the fairway?

Hitting down on the ball not only gets the ball up into the air, it also imparts backspin to help you keep the ball where it lands... preferably on the green.

Allow me a few words of interest before we go on.

Several pros I've talked to about hitting fairway shots tell me that they do actually feel that they're striking the ball with a downward thrust. Even though the swing's the same, the psychology of the game gets its due. You *should* feel as if the club action is downward. Because it *is* downward. The problem is, such a feeling can bounce around in your head and psych you into "stabbing" at the ball.

Practice is the only way you'll master this gosh-easy shot. Just don't let your head get in the way.

Hitting A Fairway Iron

I could almost copy-and-paste the text for hitting a fairway wood. The only fact worth noting is that we're assuming a fairway wood means you have an appreciable distance to go, and a fairway iron means you might be at a healthy distance or you might be within wedge distance.

Since the iron gets shorter as the distance gets shorter, and the lower-body action becomes less involved as the shot becomes shorter, you should play the ball closer to your right foot as the distance shortens. Again, the practice swings will show you the spot where you begin to brush the grass. Just play the ball about an inch behind that spot.

With an iron, expect to take a good-sized divot. The idea, of course, is to strike the ball, *then* take the divot. And that divot, incidentally, can serve as a gauge to judge your golf shot, and perhaps signal changes you should make to improve your results. Here's how:

Ideally, the divot should be about the size of a dollar-bill, and slightly thicker at the center. If the divot is too thick at the center, more than three-quarters of an inch, you might be dropping your right shoulder. If that's the case, you need to work on that aspect of your swing because a "loose" right shoulder at the top can make you hit too far behind the ball. A thin divot could mean that you're lifting up at the top or just before impact.

The divot should also tell you whether or not your swing is on target. Is the divot cut out along the target line, or does it actually point left or right? If you aren't taking a divot, you're probably not hitting down on the ball.

The other important thing about divots is that you put them back!

Tips & Tricks:
Subtle Changes That Can Help You
Work The Ball

For those times when you don't have any choice but to "work" the ball, here's what golf's legends have to say about pulling off what one old-timer, still today, calls his "trick shots."

Working the low irons (2, 3, and 4):

Most often, the need to shape a golf shot comes after you've left the tee. But not always. If you want to drive with a 2-iron, for example, playing for position and accuracy, establish a swing arc that's no different from your driver or 3-wood. Too often, the low irons are hit poorly because weekend golfers believe they must make a steeper swing arc as if they had an 8-iron in their hands.*

The same adjustments can be made on long irons to shape your golf shot, no different from any other club. You can fade the ball with a slightly open stance (dropping your left foot back), a slightly weaker grip, and a slightly outside-in

---

*Few amateurs use a 2-iron, or even a 3-iron, much less carry these clubs in their bag anymore. It's an unfortunate sign of the times. Many manufacturers are now promoting their "hybrid" clubs to replace the 2- and 3-irons. I urge you to resist this notion. The low irons are important clubs when you need distance and accuracy, or when working the ball under conditions that require maximum control.

swing. Take a slow practice swing and note the clubface position as it moves across your right foot to your left. Contact the ball with the clubface slightly open.

The adjustments to draw the ball are, as you would expect, the opposite of what we just went over. Use a slightly closed stance (drop the right foot back a couple inches or so), a slightly stronger grip, and a slightly inside-out swing. Contact the ball with the clubface slightly closed.

Count the number of times the word *slightly* was used. It's not a definitive term, of course, but remember that this section deals with subtle changes. *Slightly* and *subtle:* It's so important that you don't *over*-adjust. Little changes go a long way. Less is better than more.

Working the mid irons (5, 6, and 7):

Again, I could simply copy-and-paste the preceding text, but I would have to add a few important differences:

(1) The swing arc will not be as steep because the mid-iron clubs are shorter.

(2) Your feet are a little closer together.

(3) Your arms hang straight down, which brings your hands closer to your body and your eyes nearly over the ball.

Additionally, the swing is easier, which makes the shot more controllable. If you swing hard with these irons, you're defeating their purpose. If you feel you need to swing hard, you're clearly underclubbed.

The old pros believed that the mid irons were their "workhorse" clubs. Some would even go so far as to say that they were the most important clubs in their bag. You can't overuse them. But you can *under*use them far too often... reaching for a 9-iron when an 8-iron is the right choice.

The idea is not to impress someone with how far you can hit a 7-iron when you really stand on it. The idea is to take whatever club gets the job done with a nice, easy swing.

Easy to say, not so easy when you're on the course.

"What are you hitting, Bob?"

"I've got a 7-iron. Jerry's hitting 7, too."

"Oh."

"What did you pull out?"

"Uh, I've got a fi-ummm iron."

"A what?"

"A fi-ummm iron."

"What?!"

"A FIVE IRON! IS THAT ALL RIGHT?!"

One of my golfing friends finally got his name in the paper with a nifty hole-in-one on a tough par 3. For the next few days, he was acting as if he's Arnold Palmer. Even giving advice on how to play the hole to anyone who'd listen.

But when the weekly list of aces from courses around town appeared later in the local paper, my buddy was about to be dealt a razzing blow. After his name and course were mentioned, his listing continued with the yardage and the club used.

You're ahead of me. He made his ace on a 147-yard par 3 with a FOUR iron! He still hasn't lived it down. I should tell you, though, that the listing in the paper didn't mention his age. He's 75! Not bad for a 4-iron!

High shots, low shots:

Of all the shaping that can be done to your golf shots, particularly irons from the fairway, having the ability to hit a high approach shot can reap great benefits when you walk up on the green. A high shot means that the ball should "stick" to the green, whether you've applied good spin control or not.

To hit the ball higher than you would normally do, simply change your stance so that you're catching the ball slightly on the upswing, no different from the way you would play most tee-shots. You'll want to increase the loft of the club somewhat, by positioning your hands more to the right but never behind the ball. Where most iron shots show the hands "forward pressed," you want to minimize this "delofting of the club" in order to hit the ball higher.

Since you won't be hitting down on the ball, but *through* the ball, you should not take a divot. Instead, you'll just brush the grass at impact. Carefully note the spot where the ball should be played by making several practice swings.

Most of the legendary pros I've researched for this important shot state that they have the feeling of more wrist and arm action than lower body. Sarazen compared it to a fairway sand shot where you are trying to just "flick" the ball off the sand, assuming it's setting up nicely.

A low-flying iron shot requires basically the opposite adjustments for the high shot. You'll want to play the ball more toward the right of center to ensure catching it on the downswing. The loft of the club needs to be cut back by forward-pressing your hands (moving them forward of the ball position). In some cases, a pro will "hood" the clubface (turn it slightly inward) to further cut down on loft.

Gay Brewer, one of the best at working the ball, believed that you must be sure to lead into the shot with your hips, helping to make sure that your hands stay ahead of the ball at impact. The feeling Brewer had when making this important "punch shot" was as if he were "dragging" the clubhead through the ball because his hands were so far forward. He also noted that his follow-through was usually shorter.

Brewer was quick to note that most weekend golfers probably don't need a "bag of trick shots" and, more often than not, their efforts in trying to work the ball… well… don't work.

Working the ball requires a tremendous amount of practice. The advantages of being able to pull off these fancy shots goes without saying. But let me paraphrase what Brewer said: "If you play for pride, you probably don't need them. But if you play for a living, you must have these shots in your arsenal."

CHAPTER 6
Around The Green

"Golf is a game whose aim is to hit
a very small ball into an even smaller
hole, with weapons singularly
ill-designed for that purpose."
—Winston Churchill

Once you get to the green, or close to it, most players feel relieved. That is, assuming they haven't taken half-a-dozen strokes to get there. The reason they are relieved is because they think the hard part is behind them and the easy part lies ahead. Can you say, "Four-putt"?

So many of today's top courses are built with huge greens. It's not unusual to be 80 feet away on a 5,000 square foot green.

OK, so your course has small greens. So does mine. But nearly all the greens are elevated… no easy run-ups on my course! Yours, too? I guess that means you better be darn good with your chip shots, or, can you say, "Three-putt"?

Unwanted Advice

We all do it. We shouldn't. Even the pros do it. But they have an excuse. We don't.

I was playing a round at a fancy club on the other side of our state with the head pro in the foursome and, frankly, I was scoring well. The tendency of most average golfers when playing with a pro, especially a teaching pro, especially at a prestigious club, is to try so hard to impress this guy that their game goes straight into the toilet.

That wasn't my problem. I don't try to impress anyone. I just play my game and have fun. But the pro in our group seemed hellbent on interfering with my fun.

"You'll never be able to play this course with a grip like that, Mr. Gollehon."

"Yeah."

He didn't take the cue that I wasn't there for lessons, I was there to play and have fun.

On the 9th hole, I put a nice second shot in a shallow bunker near the green. The shot looked great from the start; it just didn't carry this thin bunker. *Oh well, I can hit out of that bunker with no problem*, I thought. Hey, I'm an optimist. On the golf course, you have to be totally positive. I walked up to my sand shot with the confidence of Tom Watson.

Only I didn't hit that shot exactly like Watson does. I play most sand shots the way Bobby Jones used to. If the ball isn't buried, if the bunker isn't deep, and I have no lip to worry about, and if the pin is at a fair distance where I can chip and run, I'll do just fine. Yes, I said "chip." I like to think of my sand shots as a chip shot.

Assuming all the parameters I listed are there for me, I play the ball as Jones would have… like a chip shot, taking a stance in the sand so that the ball is played off my right foot. That's right. My right foot. In fact, I play it a little toward the outside of my right foot. Just like the pro who never was.

I see the sand as grass and pretend I'm in the light rough. I want to hit down on the ball and get that ball up and flying before my club touches one grain of sand.

Well, the pro thought that the stance I took in the trap was a laugher. "You're not going to take a sissy shot and try to pick the ball clean, are you?"

"Not exactly," I said.

"You should open the clubface more."

"No. That's not the way I want to play this particular shot."

"Try playing it off your left foot, not your right."

"No. That's not the way I play it, either."

Just as I was ready to hit the shot, the pro offered up more advice that I don't remember today. Obviously, I was thinking more about my shot than listening to him rant about all the things he thought I was doing wrong. All I remember is that I holed that sand shot. It was so pretty and so effective. Indeed, effective. It stopped the pro cold. He said nothing. And best of all, it silenced him for the rest of the round. It couldn't have come at a better time.

And I would like to think that this young club pro learned something that day. Actually, two things: There are many different ways to make a golf shot. And there are right times and wrong times to offer advice.

This happened years ago. By now, I would like to think that he's learned the most important lesson of all: **Every golfer is an individual. The pro's job is not to make golf clones of himself.** But he's not alone. It seems to be the trend today. And a rather arrogant one at that.

The Fine Art Of Chipping

During a typical round, how many times are you on the green in regulation? Avid golfers like to keep track of such statistics. The other key stat, of course, is the number of putts. But the point of my question is to show you that even good golfers need to chip up on the green because their approach shots didn't quite find the target.

And if you play your chip shots the way the old pros used to do it, I can almost assure you that you'll have a short putt for par, maybe even a chip-in for birdie!

Today, most chip shots are played with one of the four basic wedges. It's not often anymore that you see a young player pull out a 7-iron to chip with.

The tendency today is to study the chip not from the standpoint of which club to use, but how high to loft the ball, and where the ball should land. Of course, if you have little green to work with, you'll need that wedge in order to prevent the ball from rolling too far.

A flop shot is the ultimate stop-shot, and perhaps the most difficult to master. Playing a chip from light rough with only a few feet of green to work with is the time to try it, right? Well, if you're comfortable with the shot, I guess it is. But if you haven't practiced it hundreds of times (and I doubt if you have), and if you have a relatively tight lie, play the shot the way the pros *used* to play it. Here's how:

Grab a 7-iron and take your stance with the ball positioned off your right foot. Space your feet just a few inches apart. Now turn both feet counterclockwise until they are angled at about 45 degrees to the target line. Your feet will now be pointing a little closer to the direction of where you want the ball to land. Be sure that both feet are parallel to each other.

You'll find that your swing is now easier; you've turned your body out of the way of the shot, allowing for just arm movement to accurately strike the ball. With the exception of having your feet turned to the left, you'll be chipping in much the same manner as the way you putt. Keep your elbows and wrists locked. The arms pivot from the shoulders. The head is dead still.

Let's say you're 10 to 15 feet from the green with little green to work with. You'll want to land the ball just off the green and expect it to roll to the pin. With the right speed, it will happen. And something else will happen, too. The ball will travel a true line. That's the other big advantage to this type of chip shot. **The less loft on the club**

**you select to chip with, the easier it is to hold
the target line.**

Mythconceptions About Putting

I'll never forget the first putter my company
manufactured, and particularly the trade show experience of introducing this new product to the
pro shops and retail store buyers.

The reaction was strong. We had good crowds
in our booth and many questions to answer. I must
tell you my favorites. They all lead up to the two
things that golfers apparently just don't understand
about putters. Stay with me on this.

As the prospective buyer from a big regional
chain took practice putts with our new P30, he
asked me the same question over and over.

"How is it for speed? Will this putter put me
behind the cup, like where you're supposed to be
if you miss, or will the ball just drop in the cup,
like Watson says it should?"

Here's another question that belongs in the
annals of putter bloopers.

"I have a feeling this putter is a little too fast
for the members of our club. It's an assisted-living
community, and we need equipment that will make
golf as easy as possible for them. Is there some way
you can slow it down?"

Well, I guess none of us who were staffing the booth realized that we were actually making race cars instead of putters. Trying not to be sarcastic, but not being able to turn down a good opportunity, I told both buyers that the mini-engine inside our putter would make the ball go just as fast, or slow, as they like. "The throttle is hidden in the grip," I said, with my tongue planted firmly in my cheek. And they looked at me like *I'm* stupid!

But wait, there's more.

"You know what this industry needs?" asks another buyer. "A putter that can hold the ball on line. Too many times—when I putt, anyhow—the ball veers off my intended line."

"You mean, as if the line weren't straight?" I said, trying not to giggle. "As if there were actually some break in it?"

"Yeah, that's right," says the young buyer. "You know what I'm talking about, don't you?"

See if you can believe this one.

"This putter feels heavy," says another buyer. "Will that help me find the right line?"

"Absolutely," I said. "The built-in laser-guidance system is one of our trade secrets so I'd appreciate it if you didn't tell anyone. How many do you want to buy?"

It was clear to me after wading through five days of my first PGA show that golfers are probably better off finding a good pro shop... I mean, on a golf course, to buy their stuff. But let's get to the point.

There are more golfers than you would imagine who actually expect putters, with all the fancy "technology" pumped inside, to do things that the player is supposed to do. At the risk of sounding a bit patronizing, let me make it perfectly clear that a putter will not find the right line for you and will not, miraculously, strike the ball at precisely the right speed for the chosen line and then drop the ball in the center of the cup.

No big surprise? Good. Then try this on for size:

If you hit the ball a little off line, and the ball ends up just inches to the left of the hole, I'm willing to bet that you will first check the line to make sure there were no pebbles, spike marks, or ball marks on the green that knocked that putt off that perfect line you picked.

Or, you might blame the putter.

(1) "I think the sweet spot is too small."

(2) "Did you see that? My putter scuffed the ground again."

(3) "This putter has a tendency to push the ball left."

OK. So I wanted to have a little fun with this. But I'm sure you'll agree that all golfers, even the pros, have not only blamed their putters for a bad putt, but actually got mad at them! Maybe even threw the damn things in the general direction of the next hole. Honestly, how many times have you blamed your putter, or even the golf ball itself, for a missed putt?

Putters are designed to do one thing, and one thing only: If they are used correctly, a good putter should help you keep its putterface perfectly parallel throughout the stroke. It will not twist or turn on impact; it will remain faithfully square to the line. *You're* line.

The putter will not drop off the line, either... falling ever-so-slightly toward your feet, for example, thereby missing the sweet spot when you strike the ball. It will, in every sense, give you the feeling of balance.

That's all a good putter can do. It can't figure out your line for you. It can't tell you how hard to hit the ball. It doesn't have a brain. *You* are the one with the brain. So give your putter a break... and I don't mean over the knee.

The Right Setup

- **Study your putt from all views.** While away from the ball, take practice strokes to judge speed, then step up to the ball.

- **Set the putter behind the ball, then, take your stance.**

- **Set your feet at shoulder width, parallel to the target line, with the ball positioned slightly left of the center of your stance.** If the ball is positioned too far to the left, there may be a tendency to pull the putt.

- **Make sure your weight is evenly distributed on both feet, and from heel to toe.**

- **Center the ball to the putter, using the alignment features of the putter.** You can also use the length of the putter to help you square the blade to the target line.

- **Hold the putter lightly but firmly.** Remember, "feel" comes from the fingers!

- **Bend knees slightly, and bend at the waist.** Never hunch over your putt.

- **Position your hands directly below your shoulders.** Do not forward-press your hands; doing so may close up the putterface loft and drive the ball downward into the grass.

- **Your eyes must be directly over the ball.** KEEP YOUR HEAD ABSOLUTELY STILL!

- **Find a trigger that will begin the stroke.** Use it every time. The setup routine that you follow, much as we talked about for all other golf shots, should become a natural routine for you every time you prepare to putt.

The Right Stroke

- **Pivot from your shoulders like a pendulum.** LOCK BOTH WRISTS AND ELBOWS!

- **Learn how to correlate speed with the length of your takeaway.** Short, quick strokes are rarely taught. A smooth stroke, garnering downward speed by the length of the takeaway is far more sensible. Never force the speed of your putter.

- **Allow the putter to reach its ebb on the takeaway before starting the downstroke.** Rushing the downstroke may cause the shaft to kick, throwing off your timing and speed. You must feel as if the putterhead is ready to begin its downward action before you change the force of direction.

- **Whatever you do... FOLLOW THROUGH!** Straight back, straight through. With confidence!

Tips & Tricks:
Subtle Changes That Can Help Your Putting

Don't dally over your putt:

How many seconds would you guess a pro spends over a putt before it is struck? Most amateurs would guess 10 to 15 seconds. I'll bet that the correct answer will surprise you.

From the moment you take your stance to the instant the ball is struck should take no more than six seconds. Never linger over your putt. Never waggle the putter.

Be sure that your practice strokes are not forgotten by the time you are ready to putt:

If you find that your actual stroke does not mimic your practice strokes (putts fall short, for example), try maintaining the finger tension from your practice strokes.

In other words, do not relax your grip. For some players, a regrip while addressing the ball may erase their memory of the speed gauged from their practice strokes.

Don't let a manufacturer's alignment lines confuse you:

The alignment line on many putters is merely to locate the ball to the putter's sweet spot. So-called alignment lines might not give you a true target line. Tests have been performed to determine the effectiveness of these lines. The results suggest that alignment lines would have to be at least three inches long to produce any appreciable aid in accurately lining up a putter to the target line.

I recommend using the length of the putter to align putts, setting the putter on the target line as a perpendicular.

Putters with icons to aid in alignment can be an effective aid if the overall length of the alignment aid is sufficient. The USGA, however, does not allow putter manufacturers to extend the width of a putter merely to accommodate alignment features.

Don't just practice the stroke, practice the "feel":

To get the feel of the putting stroke, swing at a good pace back and forth until you have the putter moving on a perfectly square line throughout the stroke.* This repetitive action will help you feel that the entire action comes from the shoulders. It will also show you that any other body actions can throw the putter off-line.

Putting:
The Game Within The Game

In the previous chapter, I told you that the approach shot is the most important shot in golf. Few pros would disagree... but some would. Some would say that the first putt is the most important shot in golf. Of course, you usually get to that first putt with the approach shot. It's the approach to the green that determines whether you will be chipping from grass or sand, or putting from 50 feet or five feet. I'll stand by my opinion.

Still, no one can argue that putting is crucial to making birdies. Let me tell you what seasoned pros have to say about it. And what they do that might be different from what you do.

In golf's glory days, the blade putter was the weapon of choice for most pros. From Bobby Jones' "Calamity Jane" to the infamous "Cash-In" putter, and even Arnie's trademark putter with that

---

*The length of motion for this exercise is important. The hands should swing from 15" to 20" in order to get the right action going. Shorter strokes could cause this drill to backfire. The idea is to get into the feel of a "machine-driven" putting stroke.

interesting flange that everyone copied. It was, in a sense, the first evidence of "technology."

But what was also worth noting from those days is the weight of the putter. Mostly made of brass, the weight of the putterhead was usually in the range of 12 to 15 ounces, considered "heavy" when compared to many of today's putters.

When someone asks me what features to look for in a putter, the first thing I mention is the weight. Why? Because the feel of the putter is in the weight. Even a putter that doesn't feel balanced can still feel "right" if the weight is right.

And on the subject of balance, it's really not all that difficult for a designer to achieve it. My personal preference is a center-shafted blade putter that has more height than the usual three-quarter-inch-high offerings. I like this added height for stability when putting out of short grass around the greens. A higher striking face will also prevent popping the ball by trying to get under it with a lower-profile putter. But more than that, lag putts will improve with this added face height, not so much because you have more room to strike it (just above the sweet spot), but because this added top-weight will help to start the ball rolling sooner. **A good putter gets the ball rolling right off the blade.**

Earlier, we talked about keeping the putterface square to the target. It just seems natural that putter designers would work toward improving the putter's performance to help a golfer keep the putterface square, rather than hinder that important aspect of design.

Years ago, the idea of adding weight to the toe and heel was said to help keep the putter square to the target. But this approach was, in my opinion, merely a compromise to what really helps keep the putterface square: a long-bladed putter!

To better resist putter torque (rotational forces) at impact, the putters we designed are extra long. It is the length of the putter blade that makes this noteworthy contribution. The toe/heel weighting I spoke of earlier is merely a compromise to this end, as if shortening a long-bladed putter, but adding back the weight of the material removed and locating it at the opposite poles of the putter.

Think about it. It should come as no surprise why a long-bladed putter provides better balance than compromised designs.

What better example of balance than a tight-rope walker's long pole. It's the perfect analogy to a center-supported, long-blade putter. Can you imagine how difficult it would be to balance yourself on the high-wire using a short pole? Short pole or long, can you imagine how difficult it would be if the pole were not perfectly centered?

Putters that boast some sort of weight compensation to simulate a long-bladed putter are typically called "self-aligning." Look out for this term. If the length of the putterhead is the usual three-and-a-half inches, I'd be skeptical.

Yeah, the putter is self-aligning, all right. You have to align it yourself!

Simply said, a putter has to feel good. A feeling of balance; a feeling of stability. And if you can make some putts with it, you'll have a feeling of confidence.

Confidence is the most important feeling of all.

CHAPTER 7

Playing Without Aches & Pains

Complacency among older golfers is becoming an epidemic. "The worst bankrupt in the world is the person who has lost his enthusiasm."

—*H. W. Arnold*

No instructional book on golf is complete without a chapter such as the one you are about to read. And please do read it. Even if you're a perfect specimen, in top physical condition, you need to know how to deal with nagging injuries or common ailments that strike everyone, not just the seniors, and not just the overweight and out-of-shape crowd, either.

Everyone experiences a medical problem that can greatly interfere with golf. In fact, the condition might even be caused by golf! It's a far bigger problem than most golfers imagine. The purpose of this chapter is to show you how to deal with these problems in the hope that you can continue playing, and playing well. Many physical problems do not force you to stop playing, but you will need to make adjustments in your game to stay competitive.

You'll also learn some valuable tips on how to minimize the risk of getting aches and pains as a result of the many rounds of golf you play. Interestingly enough, the golfer who does end up with a wrist or elbow injury, for example, is probably a frequent player—on the links three or four times a week—as opposed to an occasional golfer who might venture out three or four times a month!

Overuse is one of the more common reasons for joint injuries. But it isn't always the case. Heredity, lifestyles, and certainly age are all contributing factors. A smoker, for example may be more likely to receive such an injury than a non-smoker.

Adjustments To Your Game

It's not just arthritis that slows up a golfer. And arthritis, incidentally, doesn't just slow up older golfers. Especially now that members of the over-50 set are considered "seniors." Arthritis can strike at an early age and make your "tour" swing a nearly impossible challenge. Back pain is another common ailment that can strike at any age and dump your effortless swing into the tank. But you can fight back. Treating the ailment is one thing; adjusting your swing to compensate for the ailment is another.

And that's what we're going to do in this chapter, with a consensus of advice from seasoned pros who have reached those years and have learned how to make those important adjustments.

But we also have to remember that we're not just playing golf, we're playing the game of life, with all the ailments we come to expect... and many that we don't. The more we play the game, as the years roll by, the more likely we will be faced with having to make these adjustments.

Of course, changes to your basic swing might be necessary for reasons other than injury. Remember, the years do roll by. So you don't have that smooth swing you had when you were in your 30s. No big surprise. So you can't bang the ball out 250 yards anymore. Not a big surprise, either. You're growing a little shorter; your body moves a little slower, you carry Geritol in your bag, and you never miss the Lawrence Welk Show. I understand. Believe me. I'm getting to the point where I like to watch the old Welk reruns, too!

Here are some of the very basic changes you need to make in order to still enjoy yourself on the golf course and give your partner a good match, even if he's a few decades younger than you are. That's right. It's fun to beat some of these young punks out there, isn't it?

Practice backward:

No, I don't mean to swing backward, but to start your practice with your putting instead of your driving. Throw a few balls down on the putting green and practice different putts; don't keep trying to make the same putt. You only get one try at it when you're playing, so get used to practicing that way. It will help you learn how to read greens for speed and break.

I'm willing to bet that you never practiced your putting like this before. All golfers, young and old, should follow this popular wisdom from the likes of Snead, Casper, Player, and Palmer and so many other great names from an era of which many of you only caught the tail end. If only you could have seen them in their prime. But I digress. When you get older, you have a tendency to do that.

Let's move on to the chipping green and practice those short ones where you hold your arms somewhat rigid, but not tense—you know, locked wrists and elbows—a chipping stroke much like your putting stroke. Use a 7-iron and maybe a 9-iron but leave the wedges in your bag. Practice the finesse shots; try to hole every one you hit. Oh, and no sand shots to practice. Since you don't plan on hitting your ball into those nasty places, why waste your energy?

Next, you're on your way to the driving range with just three clubs: your 9-iron, 5-iron, and 3-wood. Start with your 9-iron and take a few nice, easy half-swings and see if you can make 50 yards. Gradually build up the speed and the fullness of the swing, but only to the point where you have reached a *comfortable* speed. You are not trying to kill it. Right?

The 7-iron is the next club to warm up. All full swings, all nice and easy.

Even if you like to use a driver off the tee, try the 3-wood and see if you aren't nearly as far and considerably more accurate. You should be.

There are, of course, two reasons for spending practice time before every round of golf: for the fitness of your game and the fitness of your body. You must warm up to minimize the likelihood of muscle strains or serious injury, particularly in the case of seniors. But know this: injuries on the golf course are no respecters of age or physical condition. No one should rush from their car to the first tee, tie their shoe laces and swing away. I wouldn't call that a good fitness program.

In addition to loosening up with clubs, you'll find a few good stretching exercises later in this chapter, which I hope you decide to try. Keep at least some of them in your daily repertoire. You will be surprised how much better you feel, not only on the first tee, but on the last hole, too.

Now, we don't want you to feel all used up by the time you get to that first tee, so let's set some obvious limits on the time you take to limber up. Don't spend a day there. All total, a good warm up like we just went over should take no more than 20 to 30 minutes.

Leading orthopedic surgeons believe that overuse of the driving range is a significant contributor to injury. This overuse syndrome is more noticeable in the upper extremity and lower back. Even for the pros on tour, these injuries can be traced to the repeated stress of practice.

Amateur golfers have an additional concern: They can often trace their ailments to poor swing mechanics. The combination of overuse and an improper swing can take years away from your game. So be careful.

OK. So now you know you have to be judicious with your practice sessions and the frequency of rounds you play. If you are playing several rounds per week, and feel soreness in your joints as the rounds mount, common sense would tell you to cut back. But there's more you can do.

Slow everything down:

It's sage advice not only for seniors but for all golfers who have yet to play in the U.S. Open.

Most injuries occur when you exceed a limit. Your knees, back, shoulders, elbows, and wrists have limits. And, unless you're in a longest-drive contest, there is little point in testing those limits. When tour players hook up with amateurs for a pro-am event, it's the Number One mistake they see players make. Why do they want to swing so hard, particularly if they are not normally prone to doing that? Easy question. Easy answer. They want to keep up with the pros.

The fundamental aspect of a smooth swing is the *appearance* of a slow swing. It might not really be that slow, but the fluidity of the swing makes it look like it is. And that's the way most of the pros' swings look. Obviously, Tiger's doesn't. He looks like he's going to rip the cover off the ball! But mostly, the pros have a slow-looking swing that usually baffles the amateurs. So why don't they swing as slow as the pros appear to be swinging? I think the answer, whatever it is, would include the word *frustration.*

You can slow your entire swing down, as the subhead above suggests, but a better choice would be to slow down your backswing, particularly the takeaway. Why? Because a slower backswing seems to call up a slower downswing.

Not only will you save your back, but you'll probably save some strokes, too.

Try it. Swing slowly. But don't *play* slowly. I might be in the group behind you.

You gotta hit it straight:

Whether the ravages of age or a nagging back problem that won't go away, you can make another important adjustment to your swing by setting up to hit a straight ball. Review the recommendations in chapters 3 and 4, particularly chapter 4, especially if you slice or hook the ball.

Setting up for a fade or draw is not necessarily the answer, either, because the setup changes may not be conducive to resolving your physical ailment and may actually exacerbate the problem. A nice, clean setup, and a swing that doesn't try to overpower the ball will usually get you home.

If, however, you find that you can hit a straight ball with these minor adjustments, but the distance you achieve is compromised, here are two other areas that you should consider working on:

Reprogramming the slide:

As the professional golfers age, they tend to increase the amount of slide in their lower body to gain lost power. In some cases, the slide has become so intense that a pro might seem to lose balance on the left side.

Gary Player, for example, has adjusted his slide so that he is more erect in the finish. With all the power moving to the left side, sometimes Player can be seen taking an immediate step right out of the finish and actually begin walking up the fairway.

What he's doing is trying to avoid the "comma"-shaped position after impact that we talked about in an earlier chapter. If you recall, this curved finish position is created by staying down throughout the swing.

It may be OK for younger golfers, but dubious at best for the senior set. This curving, twisting action, an integral part of the lower-body slide, exerts incredible forces on the back. For an amateur, a subtle change in the slide movement might be all that's needed. Just remember to lift up immediately after impact. And allow only the legs to slide into the shot. But even that degree of slide action should be minimized if you feel soreness in your back.

Timing of wrist, arm, and leg action in the impact zone:

As far as the upper body is concerned, more power can be developed without compromising distance if you work on that important right-arm action at the front end of the impact zone and the timing of the release of your wrists at just the right instant. As most teaching pros would tell you, you'll get the feel for this "double action" by practicing this swing adjustment slowly and in increments. Start the swing at about one-eighth speed, and progress up in eighths as you feel the swing come together.

Two of the "super-seniors" on the Champions Tour have a noticeably short backswing. Regardless of the reason—I've heard both back problems and a chronic soreness in the shoulders—they still belt that golf ball straight down the middle of the fairways. Not as far as they would like, but straight!

It's as if all the power is reserved for that final moment of impact without adding stresses to the body. The pros have accomplished the task through powerful legs that literally drive the ball out of the impact zone. Their wrist action is tweaked to perfection. And that right arm appears as if it's hammering the ball off the tee.

But it's all accomplished through timing. They've replaced stressful actions by reprogramming and tightening the sequence of motion.

What a remarkable example of swing adjustment.

A narrow stance can relieve certain stresses:

The more narrow the stance, the less likely you are to step into a back-twisting slide. The laws of physics will naturally restrict the motion and force you to lift up immediately at the finish (after the ball is on its way). If you try to slide your lower body into the ball as you normally would, the narrow stance will send you off balance.

A friend of mine, who developed severe lower-back problems from his game, was advised by his doctor to change his stance, placing his feet no more than six inches apart. It looked strange, but he was able to get decent distance even though his weight shift was now greatly restricted and his lower-body slide became nearly non-existent.

He always had a good hip and shoulder turn, which didn't seem to affect his back as much as his pronounced lower-body action. **With a new stance, he learned how to tweak his upper body**

performance. More important, he found that he could still allow his hips to start the turn but not twist to the point of pain.

His doctor told him that he would be surprised how well he could strike the ball with just his upper body and some light hip action.

Well, he *was* surprised. And so was I!

My friend certainly found the right doctor *and* the right prescription.

Retire the driver; go with your 3-wood:

Even the pros think of their 3-wood as a "more friendly" club. **Use the 3-wood off the tees, particularly on those holes with narrow landing areas, or wherever a wayward tee-shot will get you into trouble.**

The theory here is obvious, isn't it? The 3-wood is a lighter club, a little shorter, it has more loft, and it offers more control. Simply put, the 3-wood is easier on the body.

The weekend golfer's tendency to try to kill the ball is more often associated with a driver than a lowly 3-wood. And that's the other problem. Most rank beginners believe that they have to use driver to get appreciable distance. I guess that's why they're beginners.

Incidentally, this tip reminds me of a related bit of wisdom from a doctor I used to play with many years ago, who had knee problems from an old war injury. Since he had trouble keeping his knees flexed, he found that he could strike the ball more solidly by gripping down on his clubs... all of his clubs... so he went into the pro shop and asked that his clubs be cut down and regripped. Remarkably, just a fraction of an inch off his shafts did wonders.

A shorter swing arc might help you, too. Ask your pro.

Protect your wrists:

My wrists—and arms, for that matter—are thin. I'm lucky if I can curl fifty pounds. But I'm not complaining. I work on strengthening my wrists in particular, but I also know that that's the way I'm built. So I make the best of it.

Whether you have weak wrists, arthritis, or a mild wrist injury, there are several things you can do—or rather not do—on the golf course to alleviate further problems.

Taking divots on the fairway can create great shock to your wrists. A tough sand shot can do the same. And even the release of a full wrist cock on long shots can cause pain. Consider these options:

(1) In the fairways, you may want to forgo backspin and simply strike the ball at the very bottom of the swing trench. You'll have no divots to replace.

As important as a downward thrust is to producing backspin, it certainly isn't worth wrecking your wrists.

(2) If you're in the sand, and you have no lip to concern yourself with, and the ball is sitting up nicely, consider putting the ball onto the green. It's not a sissy shot, it's a smart shot.

(3) On the tees and on long fairway shots, the importance of releasing your wrists at the moment of impact has been the subject of discussion earlier in this book. Most pros believe that it's worth at least 20 yards. But, once again, a compromise is in order for those with wrist problems.

Less wrist action may not hurt you as much as you think. Why? Because the timing of the wrist release is so critical that most average golfers rarely get it right, anyhow. **Try a shorter backswing so that your wrists do not fully cock. The effects of reduced wrist action will be mitigated if you work on timing the release.**
Incidentally, all of the options noted above can also reduce the likelihood of a shoulder injury,

namely the rotator cuff. Doctors, however, believe that such injury is more often found in patients who have a weak rotator cuff to begin with, or degeneration due to age.

Yes, golfers can get "tennis" elbow, too:

We'll call it "golfer's" elbow, even though it has nothing to do with a tennis racket, although it's a similar action. It's almost a given that you'll get at least a tinge of pain in your right elbow (if you're a right-handed golfer) by hitting down on the ball with your arms instead of letting your lower body pull the club through. Some pros refer to this as "letting the arms beat the legs." If you start your downswing with your arms, you'll not only hook the ball, but you'll probably injure your elbow over time.

Always lead down with your hips, never your arms.

The other golf injury to your elbow is caused by a failure to keep a straight left arm during the backswing. If the arm bends at the top, there's a tendency to whip the arm downward by "releasing" the elbow, much as the correct action plays out for the right arm. But the "lever" action of the right arm, as we've talked about earlier, is not a contributor to injury. A similar action in the left arm, surprisingly, is. **Keep the left arm straight throughout the swing.**

For the record, these two common elbow injuries are called *medial* and *lateral epicondylitis*, respectively.

Two ways to help prevent blowing out your knees:

Sports medicine is no longer just for physicians, but for teaching pros as well. As it should be.

(1) If your pro tells you to turn your left foot out a good 20 degrees toward the target, you might think he's trying to help you make a better weight shift, and get those hips turning full, as they should. But maybe your pro is also trying to help you protect your knees.

It's a good tip. Because it accomplishes all of these things.

By turning your left foot out, it puts your foot in a stronger stance to take the added weight that builds up on the left side as you complete the swing. It takes some of the lateral stresses out of your left knee.

(2) Keeping both knees flexed throughout the golf swing is not just for swing performance, either. Most knee injuries occur when they are

locked. There's every reason to keep your knees flexed.

Consider your equipment:

Talk to your pro about your ailments or injuries in the hope that he can offer either different clubs or make changes to your existing clubs.

For example, new high-tech shafts that greatly reduce shock are Number One on the list. These shafts are usually lighter in weight and provide more flexing action for distance without the need for a power swing.

Softer, thicker grips might help, too. Again, the technology today in grip materials is quite remarkable. The cushioning effect of a soft, oversized grip goes without saying. The only drawback might be a slight loss in "feel."

Although there is some debate among doctors on the value of changing the way you grip the club, it's clear that overly strong or weak grips can be the culprit.

And then there's the matter of the golf ball itself. Do you want to hit a hard ball or a soft ball? Believe it or not, the compression rating can affect the impact on wrists and forearms, and even the shoulder joints. Try a low-compression ball.

How To Avoid Other Golf Injuries

Clearly, most of the injuries that you could receive on the golf course come from an overindulgence in playing (or practicing) or because of poor swing techniques. In fact, rankings of these injuries in medical literature do not vary by much, with back injuries leading the way. Here's a typical listing in order of occurrence:

1. Back	6. Ankle
2. Wrist	7. Hand
3. Elbow	8. Neck
4. Knee	9. Foot
5. Shoulder	10. Groin

Strange that the location of one of my injuries I received on the golf course is not on the list. I'm talking about my head. Can you guess how it happened? Let me tell you in a brief story.

Golf Round From Hell

It was a Sunday at our club, a day I rarely venture out on the course. I was there to hit a few balls on the range, testing a new theory about the ratio of hip turn to shoulder turn. It was actually an old theory, but, like anything else, old things always become new... if you give them enough time. Or just package them a little differently.

Anyhow, I was pondering whether or not I wanted to find a pick-up game and just squeeze in 9 holes. Indeed, "squeeze" is the right word on Sundays at our club; I would be competing with a course full of players. Slow players. Sunday's are family day at my place; need I say more?

I saw an old friend getting ready to load up the cart, so I wandered over to see if he minded if I joined him. Of course, no one minds. It's always more fun to play with a group. Even a twosome beats a single. I never play by myself.

"Sure! Come on and join us," he said. "Haven't seen you in a few months."

"No, that's right. It *has* been a while. Only want to play nine, though, OK?"

"Sure."

And then came the words I'll never forget.

"You don't mind if my son tags along, do you?"

"No. Of course not. Uh, that's fine. Yeah. Absolutely."

I had remembered his son from an earlier encounter. A smart-mouthed little twerp who really got on my nerves. Well, he was a little older now, all of 13, and acting as if he were a million miles away. Didn't look at me. Didn't say a word.

Danny, his dad, was the first to hit. A nice drive, in the fairway, but not long.

"Go ahead, John," he said, as he walked off the tee.

Well, I thought his son was going to hit next since he was still up there going through his practice swings.

I walked around him as if I were trying to avoid bats flying in the air. Stuck my tee in the ground, placed the ball on the tee, and then, as is customary for me, I stepped back to get a good view down the fairway of exactly how I expect my ball to travel.

BANG! Right in the back of the head! Now I know what a Big Bertha really feels like to a golf ball!

The crazy kid was swinging away without any care or concern of anyone who might get in his space.

Well, there was one good thing. Danny is a family doctor, so he knew what to do. He rushed over to me and asked me if I was OK. Actually, I was. His kid had just winged me. I didn't catch it square, thank God, or I would have been a goner.

He applied pressure to the cut to stop the bleeding, then sprayed something on it. He dashed to his bag and pulled out a bandage. (Doctors are always prepared, aren't they?)

A few holes later, with a thumping sound in my head that seemed to keep in perfect rhythm to my heartbeat, I decided that I had had enough and asked Danny to drive me back to the clubhouse.

"Gee, that's funny," says the assistant pro behind the counter, as he learns more about my accident. "We had a lady get conked in the head just last weekend on No. 8 (a short par-3). She was standing on the green while her husband was putting, and someone on the tee figured they had been there long enough, I guess."

"You mean, someone intentionally hit into them?"

"That's what we think."

And that was all I had to hear. The following year I moved to another club where I remain today, without injury, and without fear of flying objects.

(Editor's note: Golf ball injuries account for nearly 13 percent of all accidents on golf courses around the country. That's three percent more than reported for "twisted ankles." Clearly, watching where you step is the *second* most important thing to do to avoid injury. What's first? No one does it. It's too hard to hit a golf ball wearing a motorcycle helmet.)

Physical Fitness

Exercising is more than just getting into shape, or keeping in shape, it makes you feel good. And even more than that, it can help you stay fit by avoiding injury.

If you live where golf is seasonal, you should begin a progressive strategy of off-season conditioning.

Aerobic exercises, such as running, walking, swimming, or stair-climbing are important to your cardiovascular system, particularly in the case of golfers for their endurance and stamina.

Recent studies encourage stretching exercises for golfers more so than strength conditioning, particularly just before you play. These "preplay" exercises, as physical therapists call them, should include the legs and arms, and may include bending exercises, as well.

Whether or not you include back-stretching or twisting exercises is an important concern for many golfers. It's never advisable to begin an exercising program without first consulting your doctor. In some cases, you might be sent to a physical therapist who can help you set up a personal exercising program that takes your age, physical condition, and any existing problems into account.

But it's fair to say that stretching is usually the key component. Golf is a finesse game where muscular structure is not critical to performance. Few would doubt that assertion after watching golf phenom Michelle Wie, who at 13 years of age could drive a golf ball over 300 yards!

Nutrition

A good dietitian (nutritionist) or physician can help you eat the right foods, too; many work in conjunction with sports dietitians. A good rule is to avoid dietary supplements that supposedly increase metabolism or promote "fat burning." Steroid products and those containing ephedra should be avoided, and, in fact, are banned by most sports organizations. Even vitamin supplements or "health store medicines" should not be taken unless recommended by a trusted dietitian or doctor. In certain cases, excessive use can pose hidden problems, some that might develop years later.

Of particular concern to golfers are nutritional options while playing. On a hot, muggy day, it's important to take along plenty of bottled water (that's WATER, as in H_2O) and a package of pretzels to help replenish sodium lost in sweat. Potassium can also be lost in the same manner, so snacking on fruits during a round is advisable.

You'll often see pros eating a banana while playing. It's not because they're hungry; it's because they know it can help restore important minerals.

All of this is about taking care of yourself. Hopefully you'll be able to enjoy golf through your retirement because you've done those important things that will keep you going. No, I don't mean stocks or investments. I'm talking about teaching your kid golf! If you started when your son or daughter was 8 or 9 years old, and if you found a good instructor, your offspring should easily be on one of the major tours by now, making more money in one month than you made in your entire lifetime!

You supported them for all those years. Now it's their turn! Just make sure they remember to send a little something home every month. A little something to keep you in golf balls.

As I close this chapter, let me tell you that I am not an orthopedic surgeon. For that matter, I'm not a rocket scientist, either. I don't know a latissimus dorsi from a pectoralis major, and I have no clue how a 747 actually gets off the ground. But I do know golfers, and I know how important it is to be able to continue to enjoy this great game.

So if you are experiencing any problems at all, see your doctor. And it doesn't hurt any if your doctor is also a golfer. In fact, it's best if he's a degenerate golfer like you probably are. He'll understand better.

If you tell a non-golfing doctor that it hurts when you swing the club, he'll probably take a cue from Henny Youngman and tell you not to do that. He'll probably tell you to sell the clubs and take up shuffleboard.

Not exactly the answer you're looking for.

Epilogue

In your search for the best pro instructor, look for someone who has the same build, height, and weight as you do. What happens too frequently when you work with a pro who is much bigger than you are, for example, is a tendency on the part of the pro to treat you as if you are of a similar build.

The basic swing is different for a guy who's 6-foot-4 and weighs in at 230 compared to a 5-foot-11 player who only tips the scale at 170. Everything from the stance to the swing arc to the ratio of shoulder and hip turn will, or should, be slightly different, maybe considerably different.

Talk to the instructor before you begin your lessons to make sure that you feel compatibility. Ask questions. If you have anything unusual in your basic swing, and you're afraid of changing it, ask how important this uncharacteristic element of your swing is in improving your score. In other words, will the pro leave it in if it really doesn't hurt you, or will he take it out just for the sake of his own methodology. You want a pro who will be flexible and understanding, not hardened to his own methods that might only fit *him* and other golfers like him. **Remember, the idea of taking lessons is really not to improve your swing, it's to improve your scores!**

The Best Teaching Pros Are More Than Good Players, They Are Good *Teachers!*

In all fairness to golf instructors today (I've taken a few potshots at them in this book), let's make it clear just how difficult it is to teach the basic swing. Your instructor, no doubt, is a pro who can shoot scores you can only dream about. That's a given. The teacher is a good player. The question is, is he or she a good *teacher?*

The incredible task at hand is for the instructor to somehow convey in your mind exactly what it feels like to drive a ball 300 yards with an effortless-looking swing. Literally tens of thousands of golfers would love to know what it feels like. But alas, literally tens of thousands of golfers will never find out.

So how do pros convey a feeling? They can't just download the sensation from one brain port to another. At least not on *this* planet. Remember, pros have their swing so well programmed that, frankly, the feel might not be all that special to them anymore. So how can you teach something that has become so natural to you that it can't possibly be explained in words? The pros have it down to the point where they basically... well, just swing. They can't tell *that* to their students. But they *can* tell them how many swings it's taken for them to get to the point where they "just swing" and it comes off as a perfect drive nearly every time.

Of all the different sports and the challenges of teaching them, it's my humble opinion that a golf instructor has drawn the short straw. They deserve our respect as long as they show *their* respect for the challenge at hand.

Your New Objective

From this point forward, get yourself into a new mindset for this great game we all love to play. Sure, you want to go out and have fun... that's a given. But isn't it more fun to shoot a spectacular round? And you can do that. It takes practice, of course, some good advice here and there, but it really takes more than that. You need to establish a mindset that you are playing each hole to make birdie. That's your objective!

Think birdie, not par. Every shot you plan should be thought out with the goal of getting down in red numbers. Don't dwell on your ailments or adversities. Don't let any negative thoughts get in your way. Think positive, and positive things will happen.

I'm reminded of a story about a great pro who was leading a tournament that had been besieged by bad weather. The course was tough regardless of weather conditions, so he had to be sharp that morning to hold the lead to the finish line.

At the breakfast table, he was sitting with an older pro who was complaining about the weather conditions, and about the high rough, and about the way players were rushed by officials in order to finish the Saturday round before more rains came. The pro was so edgy that he had everyone else at the table on edge.

The clubhouse leader had had enough. He picked up his plate, his napkin, his utensils, and his coffee and moved over to another table. He didn't want to be influenced by the negative vibes coming from this gruff old pro.

No one wants to be around negative people. And no one should make the mistake of creating their own negatives, either. You're thinking you've got an impossible chip shot to make, a long impossible putt, a sand shot that has little chance of getting close. I don't care how good you are; if you don't think you can make it, you probably won't. It's that simple.

Surround yourself with positives.

Then go out and make some birdies!

I wish you the best golf of your life!